knitspeak

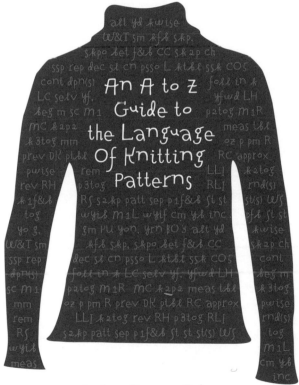

An A to Z
Guide to
the Language
Of Knitting
Patterns

Andrea Berman Price

ILLUSTRATIONS BY PATTI PIERCE STONE

STC CRAFT / A MELANIE FALICK BOOK   STEWART, TABORI & CHANG   NEW YORK

Published in 2007 by Stewart, Tabori & Chang
An imprint of Harry N. Abrams, Inc.
Text copyright © 2007 by Andrea Berman Price
Illustrations copyright © 2007 by Patti Pierce Stone

Library of Congress Cataloging-in-Publication Data:

Price, Andrea Berman.
Knitspeak : an A to Z guide to the language of knitting patterns /
by Andrea Berman Price.
p. cm.
ISBN-13: 978-1-58479-632-9
ISBN-10: 1-58479-632-4
1. Knitting. 2. Knitting--Patterns. I. Title.
TT820.P755 2007
746.43'2041--dc22
2006101805

Project Editors: Linda Hetzer and Melanie Falick
Designer: Sarah Von Dreele
Production Manager: Jacqueline Poirier

The text of this book was composed in Baufy, Interstate and Jansen.

Printed and bound in China

10 9 8 7 6 5 4 3 2 1

HNA
harry n. abrams, inc.
a subsidiary of La Martinière Groupe

115 West 18th Street
New York, NY 10011
www.hnabooks.com

Table of Contents

PART I

4-7   INTRODUCTION

8-23   PATTERN READING BASICS

PART II

24-188   AN A-Z GUIDE TO KNITSPEAK

PART III

189-223   APPENDIX

224   ACKNOWLEDGEMENTS

Knitspeak def.
A combination of words, abbreviations, numbers, and punctuation that is unintelligible to the average human and – unfortunately – to the new knitter.

Introduction

Welcome to the vast and sometimes bewildering world of knitting patterns. You are in good company if, after making a few scarves, you figured you were ready for the next step, chose a pattern, and then found yourself confused by the directions. Knitting students often say that the instructions look like they are written in a foreign language and, in a way, they are. I call this language Knitspeak.

This book is designed to help you decipher Knitspeak, which you may be surprised to learn has a real logic to it. For each symbol, term, and abbreviation that you are likely to come upon in a pattern, you will find a short explanation of what it means and what is important to know when you see it in instructions. This book gives you the tools you need to be able to read and use patterns; it is not a definitive reference guide to knitting. It is meant to live in your knitting bag so that, wherever you are, you'll never have to stop knitting because you can't understand your pattern.

Do not be alarmed if you learned a way to do something that is different than is described here. People have been knitting for centuries all over the world, and have developed tricks and techniques that they have passed on to their family members, friends, and acquaintances. Because of this, it is just about impossible to say that there is a single "right" or "wrong" way to do anything. On the other hand, if you are new to knitting and stuck, it is helpful to have one right answer to use, at least for the time being, and that is what you will find here. If you are interested, you can, of course, delve deeper into the subject by asking other knitters for help and referring to the many wonderful encyclopedic reference books available.

Using *Knitspeak*
The first section of this book gives an overview of how knitting patterns are organized and how to read them effectively. The second section gives terms in alphabetical order, starting with numbers and symbols, then abbreviations and whole phrases, spelled out. The Appendix is filled with useful tips and resources.

Getting Ready to Read Knitspeak

If you don't read anything else, READ THIS!
Following are nine tips to help make reading a pattern
written in Knitspeak easier.

1.

Before you begin a new
pattern, READ it over lightly to
get a sense of the instructions.
You may have to rely on faith that
the pattern will make sense as
the knitting develops. Take a look
at the schematic (a diagram of
the finished pieces of the project)
if one is provided. If a schematic
isn't given, try sketching out
the directions for each piece in
order to understand how the
project is constructed.

2.

COPY the pattern. Photocopying
for redistribution violates
more than a few copyright laws,
but making one copy of the
pattern for personal use is usually
acceptable. Keep the copy
in a plastic sleeve and take it out
to write notes on it.

3.

REVIEW the pattern's list
of abbreviations, and if it has
charts, the key to its charts.

4.

Scan through the pattern instructions to see if you understand most of the TERMS. Look up any that you don't know and you're immediately curious about in this book. It's not necessary to know everything before you start.

5.

If the instructions are given for more than one size, you will see numbers in PARENTHESES. Use a highlighter marker to mark the directions for the size you are making.

6.

Scan the pattern for the phrase "AT THE SAME TIME..." and highlight it.

7.

Read the FINISHING section to see if there is anything you need to know before you start.

8.

Knit a SWATCH, wash it as you plan to wash the finished project, and block it. Measure the swatch and adjust your needle size, if need be, to get the desired number of stitches per inch.

9.

Decide if there are SPECIAL TECHNIQUES or alterations you want to use throughout the pattern, such as slipping the first stitch of each row or making the sleeves 2" (5 cm) shorter, and write down these decisions on your copy of the pattern.

Pattern Reading Basics

If you are new to pattern reading, you may be confused by the ways letters, numbers, and punctuation are combined in a sentence. If knitting patterns seem more like computer code than craft to you, you are not far off. Knitspeak is a series of logical, linear operations. The instructions build line by line, like a code that tells a computer what to do, step by step.

SYNTAX

Sentences in Knitspeak are like commands and most often start with a verb and then describe the details of the command.

Here is an example of a phrase you might find at the beginning of a sweater pattern:

In Knitspeak:
CO 48
Work k2, p2 rib for 2" (5 cm), ending on a WS row.

This is what it would look like written out:
Cast on 48 stitches
Knit 2, purl 2, and repeat that sequence for the entire row. Continue in knit 2, purl 2 rib until the piece measures 2" (5 cm) from the cast-on edge. Make sure the last row you worked was on the nonpublic side of the garment, the one that will be on the inside of the sweater when it is worn. You should be ready to knit a right-side row (the public side) at the next line of instructions.

Pay attention to closing statements like "ending on a wrong side row" because the next set of instructions will assume that you will be starting from that point. Or you might find a closing statement like "Increase 7 stitches evenly across row (98 stitches)." This is a reality check, i.e., when you have finished increasing, you should have 98 stitches. This way, you can check your work before you go any further.

PUNCTUATION

Commas, asterisks, and parentheses are used to set apart repeated actions that are part of a larger set of instructions. Here is an everyday example that may sound silly, but it shows how a simple action would be translated into the syntax of Knitspeak:

An everyday example:
Make a shopping list. Bring it to the store.
Go through the aisles, *find item, put in
shopping cart, repeat from * until all items
on your list have been loaded into the cart.

Here is a similar example in Knitspeak:
Cast on 60.
*Knit 4, purl 6, repeat from * to end of row.

Do not be put off if you cannot visualize the result in your head the first time you encounter this kind of sentence in a pattern. Sometimes you have to take it one line at a time, and trust that when you see how the knitting develops, it is likely to make more sense.

Pattern Name

A) PHOTO

B) SIZES

C) MATERIALS

D) GAUGE

**E) STITCH PATTERNS
AND/OR NOTES**

F) INSTRUCTIONS

G) FINISHING

H) CHART

I) SCHEMATIC

J) ABBREVIATIONS

PATTERN FORMAT

A pattern can be divided into parts for a clearer understanding.

A) PHOTO

Sometimes the photo of the item will help you figure out the instructions. For example, a sweater photo may help you understand the intended fit, neckline style, and sleeve type, as well as how pieces are attached to each other once they are finished.

B) SIZES

This section tells you the sizes for which instructions are given. Letters like S, M, L, and XL may be given or the sizes may be given in finished measurements only. If the sizes are given as S, M, L, and XL, always check the finished measurements also, as the pattern writer's idea of a certain size may not match yours. If only one measurement is given for a sweater, it will be the chest/bust measurement. The measurements given are the finished measurements of the garment, which are typically larger than the actual body measurements of the intended wearer. The difference is called **EASE**.

C) MATERIALS

This section tells you what kind of yarn, needles, and notions you need for the project. If you cannot find the yarn indicated in the pattern, you can substitute another one that is similar. Finding the right yarn requires an awareness of the properties of different yarns and a sense of artistry, as well as good judgment. *See Guidelines for Substituting Yarns on page 192.*

D) GAUGE

This section tells you at which gauge you need to knit—that is, how many stitches and rows per inch of knitted fabric—in order to create an item of the desired size. To knit at the specified gauge, you may need to use needles larger or smaller than the pattern's recommended size. *For more on this topic, see Gauge on page 81.*

E) STITCH PATTERNS AND/OR NOTES

A set of instructions may be given in a separate box for a sequence of stitches that make up a pattern. The instructions may direct you, for example, to "Knit in Pattern A for 4" (10 cm)," so you would follow Pattern A in the box for that section. The same stitch pattern may also be shown on a chart.

In addition, notes may be given on how the project is constructed. These notes may be general or specific, depending on the pattern writer's style and the complexity of the project.

F) INSTRUCTIONS

Instructions can be given row by row in prose; they can be visual, with schematics, charts, and photos; or they can be any combination of these elements.

Some people need to visualize how an item is taking shape before they can understand written instructions. Others work better by reading line by line and watching the item develop as they go. If you prefer visuals and your pattern has few, try using graph paper to sketch out the directions. If you prefer prose, but the pattern has a lot of charts, you may want to write out the instructions line by line.

At the beginning of the instructions, the pattern may list notes that apply to the entire pattern. Don't hesitate to make additional notes on the pattern to make it more understandable.

G) FINISHING

The section on finishing (or "making up") describes how the project will be assembled once the pieces are complete. It is important to read this section before you begin, as it may have implications for the way the project is knitted.

H) CHART

A chart is knitting directions shown in a grid format using symbols (for which a key is usually given) instead of words. *See Guidelines for Reading Charts on page 55.*

I) SCHEMATIC

Often patterns include a diagram—called a schematic—showing the shape and finished measurements of the pieces of the project. *For more on this topic, see Schematic on page 149.*

J) ABBREVIATIONS

Patterns sold individually usually include a list of the abbreviations they use. Most books and magazines contain a list for the publication as a whole. While some abbreviations are in common use through most parts of the industry, many are not standardized. This book contains explanations of the most commonly used abbreviations. Always review the abbreviations list and key that come with a pattern, as the definitions they contain will naturally supersede those in this book if they are different.

COMMON PATTERN
CONVENTIONS

Directions for different sizes
Patterns are often written so that one set of directions covers several sizes,
which can result in long strings of numbers that are challenging to read.
Parentheses are used to separate instructions for the smallest size from
additional sizes. *See ( ) Parentheses on page 26.*

Directions for similar pieces
Sometimes pattern writers save space by giving instructions for two similar
pieces at the same time, such as a sweater back and front. The directions are
given in their entirety for the back and, for the front, will say something like
"Work as for back until piece measures 17" (43 cm)." You will then find
specific instructions for any section of the front that is different than the back.

Directions where shaping is reversed
Many patterns give the entire set of instructions for one side of the front
of a cardigan or a neckline, and then direct you to reverse shaping when
working the other side. In a case like this, if you feel the need for
more specific instruction, you can write out the reversed instructions for
the second side, line by line, or you can create a **SCHEMATIC** on graph
paper to help you visualize how the shaping will go on the other side.
For example, suppose the left front is worked first, with instructions like
"dec 1 st at neck edge every 4 rows 14 times." This means decreasing
at the *end* of right-side rows. To reverse shaping for the right front,
you'd decrease at the *beginning* of right-side rows.

Directions for several sizes or gauges in fill-in-the-blank format
Some patterns are written out in sentences, but blank spaces are left in
places where you need to fill in the correct number for the size or gauge
you are making.

Here is an example of a fill-in-the-blank type of layout:

Back of Sweater	Women's Sizes		
	S	M	L
Cast on _____ stitches	72	76	80
work in knit 2, purl 2 ribbing for 2" (5 cm).			
Increase _____ stitches at the beginning	0	1	2
of next 2 rows.			

In this example, you would cast on 72, 76, or 80 stitches (depending on your size), then increase 0 stitches at the beginning of each of the next 2 rows for the small size, 1 stitch for the medium, and 2 stitches for the large.

THE WAY WORDS ARE USED IN KNITTING PATTERNS

As in any language, Knitspeak contains words that mean different things depending on context. For example, you might tell a friend that you are sitting on the front porch knitting, when in fact you are knitting and purling. In this case you are using the word knitting in a general way. At the yarn store, you might ask a knitting teacher, Should I be knitting or purling in this section? In this case, you are using the same word to mean making a knit stitch. To get around this, many patterns use the word *work* instead of *knit*. To work means to make stitches; these stitches could be knit or purl. For example, work in knit 1, purl 1 rib means to alternate knitting and purling in the same row. For more on words with multiple meanings, *see Knitspeak Doublespeak on the next page.*

Knitspeak Doublespeak

In Knitspeak, as in any language, words can have different
meanings depending on the context in which they are used.
Following are some common examples.

Knit

1. To create fabric using knitting needles, as opposed
to a crochet hook or a loom

2. To create a knit stitch, as opposed
to a purl stitch

Pattern

1. The set of instructions for creating a knitted item

2. A combination of stitches that creates a certain knitted
fabric, as in stitch pattern

Stitch

1. One loop of yarn on your needles

2. A way of manipulating the loops of yarn on your needles—for example, a knit stitch, a purl stitch, or a yarn over

3. Another way of saying stitch pattern—for example, Seed stitch and Stockinette stitch are the names of two stitch patterns

Seam

1. As a verb, seam means to sew up

2. As a noun, the seam is the place where two pieces are sewn together

Weave

1. To tuck the ends into the wrong side of the knitting

2. A technique for securing long pieces of yarn (called floats) when working with more than one color in a row

3. Techniques for joining two pieces of knitted fabric

Right side

1. The outside or public side, in contrast to wrong side or nonpublic side

2. The right side, as opposed to left side. When used in this sense, right side refers to the wearer's right side, not the viewer's right side

WHAT KNITTING PATTERNS
DO NOT TELL YOU

Some information is not included in patterns because the pattern writer assumes the knitter knows these things or will apply her or his own creativity to the work, or because there isn't enough space to include every detail. Experienced knitters have a good sense of where to add and alter, but beginners and intermediates may not even know that options exist.

This book includes many of these tips and tricks in the alphabetical listing of terms beginning on page 25.

To get you started, here are some of the most common assumptions:

Bind off in pattern unless otherwise indicated
Patterns do not always specify, but for best results, bind off in the pattern you are working. In other words, if you are working a pattern of knit 2, purl 2, either knit or purl each stitch before you bind it off, just as if you were continuing to work without binding off. *For more bind-off tips, see page 46.*

Knit separately means add in a new ball of yarn
To knit two sections separately, you have to add in a new ball of yarn so that each section may be knit from its own ball. For example, add a new ball at the base of a V-neck so that you can knit the right front and the left front of a sweater at the same time, alternating one row in one section from its ball with one row of the other section from the other ball. *See At the same time.*

Finishing techniques are employed throughout the knitting, not just at the end
There are techniques that knowing knitters use to make their finished products look great and fit well. Some of these finishing techniques must be planned at the beginning, such as working increases and decreases a couple of stitches in from a piece's edges to leave smooth edges for easier seaming. Some designers include these techniques in their patterns as a matter of course while others give only the basic requirements and leave it to the knitter to decide whether or not to include these niceties.

Block the pieces before sewing seams

Most patterns simply say sew seams. Before you sew, however, you should weave in any ends that you are not going to use to sew seams. Then block each piece to the size and shape shown in the pattern's schematics, to ensure the finished garment fits correctly. Blocking also tames curling edges, making the seaming process easier. *See Block.*

PATTERNS AS MANDATES, PATTERNS AS GUIDELINES

At times, you may not think a pattern makes sense. However, if you follow the directions as they are written, your confusion will probably resolve itself as you see the design take shape. For the most part, a pattern represents the pattern writer's best thinking on how to make the item. Patterns are tempered, however, by available publication space, by publishing conventions, by the designer's personal preferences, by preconceptions of the knitter's abilities, and by other factors. For this reason, as you become more accomplished you may see alternate approaches. You may decide to look upon patterns not as mandates that must be followed, but as guidelines from which to depart.

ERRATA

If you have diligently tried to follow the directions as written, but you are still confused, it may not be your fault. Look on the publisher's or designer's website for a list of corrections to errors in the pattern, called errata. If you search the Internet you may also find knitters who have worked on the same project and are able to help you.

HELPFUL HINTS FOR KEEPING
TRACK OF PATTERN INSTRUCTIONS

Following are some tips for keeping track of what you are doing while you are knitting. Pick and choose the ones that you think will be helpful on a project-by-project basis.

To keep track of the number of stitches you are casting on

Weave waste yarn in a contrasting color into your knitting as you cast on. This is especially handy when you are casting on a large number of stitches. Cast on 10 stitches, then lay the waste yarn over the working yarn from front to back, leaving a short tail in the front of the work and letting the rest dangle down the back. Cast on another 10 stitches, and bring the yarn to the front again. Continue moving the waste yarn between back and front every ten stitches as you cast on so you get a horizontal line of waste yarn that marks off your stitches in groups of ten. Once you have cast on and checked that you have the right number of stitches, pull out the waste yarn.

To keep track of the number of stitches in each pattern repeat

Place stitch markers at the end of each repeat of your stitch pattern—for example, if your stitch pattern repeats every 12 stitches, then place a stitch marker after every 12th stitch. Note that some lacework has stitch sequences that cross over repeat boundaries, in which case you may have to shift your stitch markers.

To keep track of the number of rows so you do not have to count later

Row counters

Use a barrel-shaped row counter that fits on the needle and move the dial each time you finish a row. Or keep a golf-scorer or kacha-kacha counter close by and remember to change the number every row.

Safety pins
Attach a safety pin to the work every 5 rows as you knit. Then you will
be able to count the pins, knowing each represents 5 rows.

To keep track of "special" rows
Sometimes you need to do something special once every few rows—for
example, work sleeve increases once every 6 rows, work V-neck decreases once
every 4 rows, or cross a cable once every 8 rows. The following tricks can
help you keep track of these special rows.

Safety pins
If you need to work a specified number of special rows, create a chain contain-
ing one safety pin for each special row. For example, if a sleeve pattern says to
increase every 6 rows 17 times, attach a chain of 17 pins to your knitting.
Every time you increase, place a pin on the side of that row. When you have
used all the pins, you will have completed all 17 increases.

Waste-yarn marker, woven into knitting
On your first special row, lay a piece of waste yarn over your knitting from
front to back, between the needle tips, leaving a short tail in the front of the
work. On the next special row, bring the waste yarn to the front. Continue
weaving the waste yarn back and forth on each special row. Count the number
of times it runs through the knitting to count the increases, decreases, or cable
crosses. Work to the point above the waste-yarn marker, spread your knitting
apart slightly, and count the horizontal bars above the waste yarn to count
the number of rows since your last increase, decrease, or cable cross.

If you are making a sleeve, run the waste yarn up the middle of the piece
so that when you get to the top, the waste yarn marks the exact center of
the sleeve.

Waste-yarn markers, tied to knitting
Use short pieces of waste yarn in a contrasting color as markers. For example, if a pattern calls for increases on the sides of a sweater to be done five times, tie a piece of waste yarn into each row where you made an increase. When you have five markers tied into your knitting, you have completed the increases.

To keep track of details
There are a number of ways to remind yourself where you left off in the pattern or what changes you have made to a pattern. This is especially helpful when making two of a kind, such as for sleeves, socks, and mittens.

Copy and write on the pattern
Make a copy of the pattern and put it in a plastic page protector along with a piece of notepaper. This way your notes and sketches stay with the pattern.

Keep a knitting journal
Keep all of your notes together in a bound book, a three-ring binder, or a spiral notebook.

Price tags
Write notes on cardboard tags with strings (available at office supply stores) and tie them onto your knitting.

To keep track of charted patterns or row-by-row directions

Typing stand or chart holder
This is a stand that holds a page upright, with a magnetic ruler that you can move up and down (sold at office supply and craft stores).

Sticky notes
Place a sticky note on the chart above the row you are working so you can see how the current row relates to the previous rows.

Index Cards
When working stitch patterns that you find hard to memorize, write out the sequence or chart for each row on an index card. Make one card for each row of the repeat. Punch a hole in the corner of the cards and secure them with a locking notebook ring so you can flip them. Put a rubber band around the stack to mark your place when you put your knitting down.

Beads
If you are working a sequence you have memorized but you need to remember which row you have completed, thread beads equal to the number of rows in a repeat on a piece of rawhide or thick twine so they do not easily slide, and move them from one end of the twine to the other as you work each row.

To keep track of simultaneous changes

Checklists can help you keep track of simultaneous changes, such as sections of a pattern that include the phrase *at the same time*. See page 35 for an example of a checklist for simultaneous decreases at the arm and neck edges of a sweater.

An A-Z Guide to Knitspeak

24-29	**SYMBOLS**
30-188	**A-Z**

[ ] Brackets

✳ Asterisk

Brackets are used to separate short sections of pattern instructions that are to be worked as a group a specified number of times. Sometimes parentheses are used for the same purpose.

An everyday example:
Walk the dog to the park and find a stick. Pick up a stick and throw it about ten yards/meters from the dog. When the dog returns with the stick, [pat the dog's head] twice, and give the dog a treat.

In this example, when the dog brings back the stick it gets its head patted twice but only gets one treat.

An example in Knitspeak:
Row 3: K5, [k2tog] 3 times, k5.

This is what it would look like written out:
For Row 3, knit 5 stitches, then knit 2 stitches together 3 times, then knit 5 stitches.

(as in repeat from ✳ or repeat from ✳ to ✳)
Asterisks are used to define a sequence of actions that are to be repeated. Only the directions following or inside the asterisks are repeated.

An everyday example:
Walk the dog to the park and find a stick. *Pick up the stick. Throw the stick about 10 yards/meters from the dog. When dog returns with the stick, pat the dog's head. Repeat from * until dog is tired.

In this example, you would repeat the whole sequence from picking up the stick to patting the dog's head until the dog gets tired.

An example in Knitspeak:
*K2, p2, repeat from * across row.

This is what it would look like written out:
Knit 2 stitches, then purl 2, and repeat until you have used up all the stitches in the row.

( ) *Parentheses*

Parentheses are used to indicate measurements, yarn requirements, or instructions for different sizes in one pattern. Parentheses are sometimes used in combination with brackets when both imperial and metric measurements are provided. Once you have selected the size you are making, you will find the corresponding directions for that size inside or outside the parentheses (or brackets). In the example below, you can see that the directions are given for three sizes. Yarn requirements and knitting instructions are given in the same order, with the small size first, then the medium and large sizes.

This means for a 38" (96.5 cm) chest, you will need 6 skeins worsted-weight wool and will cast on 104 stitches. You would follow the directions for the second number inside the parentheses throughout the directions. It's a good idea to go through the pattern and highlight or circle the numbers for your size before you start knitting.

Finished Measurements
34 (36, 38)" (86.5 [91.5, 96.5] cm) chest

Yarn
5 (5, 6) skeins worsted-weight wool (172 yards [157 m] each)

For sweater back, CO 96 (100, 104) sts.

O Zero

A pattern might contain a sequence of numbers that includes a zero. This happens when instructions for several sizes are included in one set of directions. If you find a zero given for the size you are making, there is no need to do anything.

For example:
At beginning of next 2 rows, inc 1 (0, 1) stitches for a total of 20 (22, 24) stitches.

In this example, if you were making the middle size, you would knit the next 2 rows without increasing *any* stitches at the beginning of each row.

1x1 Rib/2x2 Rib

See Rib/Ribbing.

Chart Symbols

Chart symbols have not been standardized by the knitting industry so there can be variation from pattern to pattern; however, the symbols given here are very common.

SYMBOL	ABBREVIATION	MEANING
☐ or Ⅰ	k	Knit on right side, purl on wrong side
• or –	p	Purl on right side, knit on wrong side
V	sl	Slip purlwise with yarn held to wrong side
O	yo	Yarn over
⊠ or M	M1	Make 1
Γ or ⊠	RLI	Right lifted increase
⅂ or ⅄	LLI	Left lifted increase
ⱴ	k1f&b	Knit into front and back of next stitch
⟋ or ∕	k2tog	Knit 2 together on right side, purl 2 together on wrong side

SYMBOL	ABBREVIATION	MEANING
⟋ or ⟍	ssk	Slip, slip, knit on right side; slip, slip, purl on wrong side
⟋ or ⟋	k3tog	Knit 3 together on right side, purl 3 together on wrong side
⟋ or ⟍	sk2p	Slip 1, knit 2 together, pass slipped stitch over
⋀ or ⋀	s2kp	Slip 2 as if to k2tog, knit 1, pass slipped stitches over
⟋⟍ or ⊔⊓	2/2 RC	2-over-2 right cross: slip 2 sts to cn and hold at back, k2, k2 from cn
⟋⟍ or ⊓⊔	2/2 LC	2-over-2 left cross: slip 2 sts to cn and hold at front, k2, k2 from cn
■	n/a	No stitch

A

Acr – **Across**

On straight needles, work across means to work all the stitches of an entire row.

If the directions say to work across 12 stitches, work those 12, then follow the next set of directions.

If you are knitting in the round using double-pointed needles, work across 3 needles means to work all the stitches on all 3 needles.

Add new ball of yarn
See Attach a new ball of yarn.

Alt – **Alternate**

Most commonly used to mean alternate row. This means you would only perform the operation every other row.

American style
See below.

Approx – **Approximately**

....

American style

Also called English style, right-hand carry, or right-handed knitting, American style refers to a common style of knitting in which the knitter holds the working yarn in the right hand. It is also sometimes called throwing because of the movement of the right hand as it loops the yarn around the needle. This is in contrast to the CONTINENTAL STYLE of holding the yarn in the left hand, also known as picking.

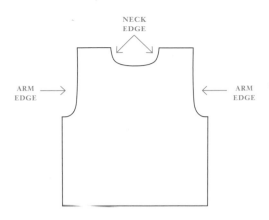

ARM EDGE → ← ARM EDGE

NECK EDGE

Arm edge

The arm edge is the edge of the garment closest to the armhole or shoulder; this is used most often in contrast to NECK EDGE.

As established

This means that a pattern has already been described in the directions; you would continue to work in that pattern until the directions tell you otherwise.

In Knitspeak, a pattern might say:

> *Rows 1-3:* K
> *Rows 4-6:* P
> Cont as established until piece meas 5" (12.5 cm).

This is what it would look like written out:

> Knit 3 rows, then purl 3 rows, then continue alternating 3 rows of knit with 3 rows of purl until the piece measures 5" (12.5 cm).

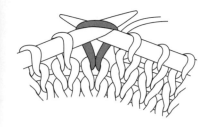 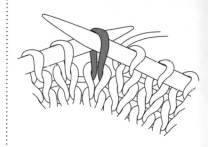

As if to knit

This phrase means to insert your needle as you would to make a knit stitch; it often follows directions to slip (or transfer) stitches from one needle to the other (i.e., slip as if to knit). In this case (and as shown above), you would guide the needle under the front leg of the stitch from the front of the work to the back, holding the yarn to the wrong side unless the instructions indicated otherwise.

As if to purl

This phrase means to insert your needle as you would to make a purl stitch; it often follows directions to slip (or transfer) stitches (i.e., slip as if to purl). In this case, you would guide the needle under the front leg of the stitch from the back of the work to the front, holding the yarn to the wrong side unless the instructions indicated otherwise.

KNIT STITCH   PURL STITCH

As they appear

This means to knit the
knit stitches and purl
the purl stitches.
The two stitches make
different shapes: a knit
stitch forms a V, while
a purl stitch forms a
short, horizontal bump.
If you see a V, knit;
if you see a horizontal
bump, purl.

Asterisk
*See * on page 25.*

KEEPING TRACK OF
SIMULTANEOUS SHAPING

When shaping two parts of a piece at the same time—for example, the shoulder and back neck of a sweater—a checklist can be helpful. Read through the pattern instructions and create a checklist for your size on lined paper or in a spreadsheet, with one row in the checklist for each row of knitting. Note in the checklist the shaping that must occur on each row. Then check off each row as you knit it.

The following is an example of pattern instructions for simultaneous decreases at the arm and neck edges of a sweater, given first in Knitspeak and then in checklist format.

Knitspeak format

Bind off 4 (5, 6) stitches at arm edge every other row 5 times, and at the same time, decrease 1 stitch at neck edge every 4 rows 1 (2, 2) times.

At the same time

This phrase means that you are to carry out two operations at the same time. You will find it often in sweater or vest patterns where you decrease for the armholes on one edge and, at the same time, you begin to shape the neck.

Checklist format

Note that the checklist is read from the bottom up.

FOR SIZE MEDIUM			
WRONG-SIDE ROWS	NECK EDGE	ARM EDGE	RIGHT-SIDE ROWS
Row 10			
		BO 5	Row 9
Row 8	Dec 1		
		BO 5	Row 7
Row 6			
		BO 5	Row 5
Row 4	Dec 1		
		BO 5	Row 3
Row 2			
		BO 5	Row 1 START HERE

Attach a new ball of yarn

There are many ways to attach a new ball of yarn. Here are two easy methods:

Drop the end of the old yarn, leaving a 6-8" (15-20.5 cm) tail, and begin knitting with the new one. If you like, make a loose square knot with the two tails to keep them from unraveling; later, untie the knot before weaving in the ends in opposite directions. Whenever possible, attach a new ball of yarn at the edge so you do not create a bump in the middle of a row.

If you are knitting with a yarn that is thinner than worsted weight and the location of the switch will not be noticeable, hold the two strands together with the tails pointing in opposite directions and knit with the two strands held together for a few stitches. On the next row, knit the two strands of each doubled stitch as one.

See Work(ing) both sides at once for an illustration of where a new ball is attached when working shoulders separately.

Attached I-cord

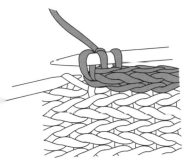

A form of I-cord used as an edging, so called because you attach it to a fabric edge as you knit it. To work 3-stitch attached I-cord, cast 3 stitches onto a double-pointed needle. *Slide the stitches to the right end of your double-pointed needle. Pull the working yarn snug across the back of the work. Knit 2, slip 1 knitwise with yarn in back, pick up and knit a stitch in the fabric edge, and pass the slipped stitch over the picked-up stitch. REPEAT FROM * *(see Asterisk entry on page 25) along the fabric edge.*

B

Back

"Back" can mean multiple things, depending on context.

It can refer to the back piece of a project, such as the back of a sweater or the back of a pillow.

It can refer to the side of your work that faces away from you as you are knitting. For example, "slip purlwise with yarn in back" means to hold the yarn to the back side of the fabric (the side facing away from you) while you slip a stitch AS IF TO PURL.

And the "back loop" of a stitch is the part of a stitch on the far side of your needles.

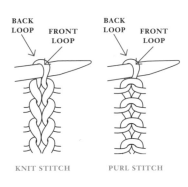

BACK LOOP   FRONT LOOP   BACK LOOP   FRONT LOOP

KNIT STITCH   PURL STITCH

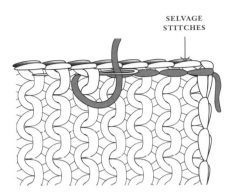

SELVAGE STITCHES

Backstitch

A sewing technique that creates a strong, inelastic seam.

To backstitch, line up the two edges of knitting with right sides together. If helpful, use pins or clips to hold the pieces together while you sew.

With a threaded **YARN NEEDLE**, take one or two "anchor" stitches at the right edge, leaving a 6-8" (15-20.5 cm) tail. Make the stitches just under the selvage stitches.

Insert the needle through both thicknesses of fabric to the right of the anchor stitches, and bring the needle up through both layers of knitting one or rwo stitches to the left of the anchor stitch; pull the yarn through.

Continue stitching by inserting the needle down through the same point where your yarn came up on the previous stitch, and bringing it to the front and to the left of that point. At the left edge, fasten off and **WEAVE IN ENDS**.

You can use this method of seaming if you have made a garment too wide and want to take in the width. To do this, make the seam in farther, away from the selvage.

Backwards loop cast-on

Also known as the e-wrap cast-on, this is an especially easy way for beginners to put their first row of stitches on the needle. However, knitting the first row after the cast on can sometimes be tricky for beginners for two reasons: The cast-on stitches can easily become loose at this point, and are angled in such a way that it takes some fiddling to insert the working needle into them.

This cast-on method is more often used to add stitches to knitting that is in progress. For example, when knitting mittens, a common procedure is to knit a tube, place several stitches onto a holder, and use the backwards loop cast-on to replace the same number of stitches so you can continue knitting the tube. The stitches on the holder are worked later to create a thumb.

To cast on if you are starting from scratch, begin with a SLIP KNOT on a needle, pulling until the loop is snug but not tight. Hold this needle in your right hand fairly close to the tip, holding the knot in place as you grasp the needle. The slip knot counts as your first stitch. For each additional stitch, follow steps 1-3.

If you are adding stitches to knitting in progress, hold the needle with the stitches in your right hand, then repeat steps 1-3 for each stitch.

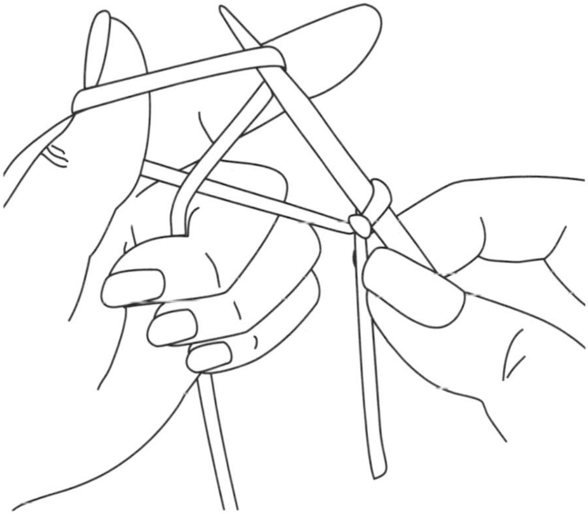

---

step 1
Wrap the yarn from the ball around your left thumb from front to back, and hold it secure with your other fingers.

step 2
Bring the tip of the needle up under the yarn alongside your thumb as shown in the illustration above.

step 3
Slip your thumb out of the loop and tighten the loop on the needle so it is snug but not tight.

You may find that the stitches have a tendency to twist around the needle; just re-align them if you need to, before knitting, by turning them so the knot side is facing down.

BALL

SKEIN

HANK OR TWISTED SKEIN

Ball vs. skein vs. hank

These terms describe the form the yarn is in when you purchase it.

A ball is ready to knit: One end is usually wrapped around the ball under the label; the other end is tucked away inside the center of the ball. You can use either end (or both!) but pulling from the center keeps the ball from rolling around a lot as you work. To find the end in the center, probe the ball's core with your finger and pull out the inner-most thread. A small tangle of yarn usually comes with it.

The word skein (rhymes with rain) is sometimes used to refer to a tube of yarn that is ready to knit, and other times is used to mean a long circle of yarn that has been twisted into a figure eight for easier storage and must be wound into a ball before knitting. The words hank and skein are often used interchangeably.

If your yarn is in a hank or twisted skein, you will need to wind it into a ball. To wind by hand, pull the yarn out of its figure eight shape and arrange it around the back of a chair or onto another person's outstretched hands. Undo the knots or ties that hold the yarn strands together in place, and wind the yarn into a ball, being careful not to wind so tightly the yarn stretches. Alternatively, yarn stores often have an apparatus with rotating arms called a yarn swift, which, when used with another gadget called a ball winder, makes short work of winding.

Bar
*This is the horizontal
length of yarn that
connects one stitch to
the next. See Stitch.*

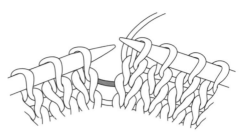

. . . .

Ball band
This is another term for yarn label.
See page 196.

Bar
See above.

Bar increase
Bar increase usually refers to **K1F&B**,
knitting into the front and back
of the next stitch, as this produces a
distinctive horizontal bar of yarn at
the increase. Some patterns, however,
use bar increase to mean Make 1,
abbreviated as **M1**, since Make 1
is worked into the horizontal strand
or "bar" of yarn between 2 stitches.
To determine which meaning
your pattern intends, refer to its
abbreviations list, or study the

pattern or photo to determine if
each increase is worked *in* a stitch,
creating a visible horizontal bar
(indicating K1f&b), or *between* two
stitches, creating an inconspicuous
increase (indicating Make 1).

Beg – **Beginning**

Being careful not to twist
See Join, being careful not to twist.

Bet – Between

Bind off
See BO.

Block
Blocking is a way of "setting" the knitting, evening out the stitches, and helping the knitted piece to lie flat; directions may also say block lightly or block to measurements. Blocking can also be used to manipulate the shape of the finished piece. Blocking is most often done after weaving in the ends but before sewing the pieces of a garment to each other.

Several blocking methods exist. Steam-blocking is a simple method that works well for natural fibers such as wool, but its extreme temperatures can cause synthetic fibers to droop or even melt; check your yarn label or practice on a test swatch to determine if your yarn can withstand steam-blocking.

To steam-block to size, lay the knitted piece on a clean bedspread, carpet, or large towel. Using rustproof pins, pin the piece to desired measurements. Steam, hovering the iron over but not pressing the fabric. If necessary, impart more steam by placing a damp cloth (such as a washcloth) over the knitted piece, and pressing the cloth lightly. Allow the fabric to lay flat until dry. Do not block ribbing or any parts that need to retain their elasticity.

You can find more information on blocking in books and on websites under the word *finishing*.

BO – Bind off

Binding off secures the last row of knitting, closing the loops so that the stitches will not unravel.

If the instructions do not indicate the type of bind off to use, here is the simplest method. Always bind off slightly looser than you normally knit so that the knitting does not pucker or pull in.

step 1
Work the first stitch.

step 2
Work another stitch. You now have 2 stitches on the right-hand needle.

step 3
Slip the left-hand needle into the right-most stitch on the right-hand needle.

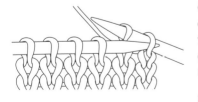

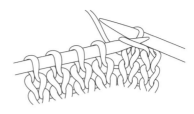

step 4
Pass the right-most stitch over the left-most stitch and off the right-hand needle.

step 5
You now have 1 stitch on the right-hand needle.

Repeat steps 2 through 5 until no stitches remain on the left-hand needle and you have 1 stitch on the right-hand needle.

Cut the yarn, leaving a 6-8" (15-20.5 cm) tail. Slip the last stitch off the knitting needle, bring the tail through the stitch, and tug gently to close the loop. **WEAVE IN END** and trim off excess.

See *Bind Off Tips* on next page.

bind off Tips

1

Always bind off looser than you normally knit. If you are a tight knitter, use a needle one or two sizes larger to keep the bind off from puckering.

2

Bind off in pattern (*see BO in patt*) unless directed otherwise.

3

If the instructions say to bind off 5 stitches, you will actually be working 6 stitches; 5 are going to be bound off, and the sixth remains as a loop on your right-hand needle.

4

When binding off in the middle of your knitting, don't count the stitches you knit; instead, count each time you pass one stitch over another and off the right-hand needle, as described in step 4 on page 45.

5

When binding off at the end of a piece, when 1 stitch remains on each needle, slide the last loop from the right-hand needle to the left-hand needle and knit the stitches together. This helps keep the last bound-off stitch from becoming overly large and loopy.

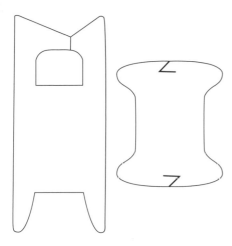

Bobbin
Spool or other device used for winding lengths of yarn for knitting with multiple colors.

BO in patt – **Bind off in pattern**
This means that as you make the stitches that you are about to bind off, you work them in the manner called for in the pattern. For example, if you were working in knit 2, purl 2 rib, you would knit the knit stitches and purl the purl stitches across the row as you bound them off.

Bobble

A bobble is a bubble-like bulge worked into the knitted fabric. It is created by making several stitches out of one stitch, adding a few rows to give it bulk, and then gathering them back in again to create a round bump.

For example, to create a 5-stitch bobble, knit 5 stitches into 1 stitch by knitting into the front of the stitch and then into the back leg of the stitch, knitting again into the front leg, and again into the back, and once more into the front. Turn your work around so you are working on the wrong side (WS) of the fabric, and purl the 5 new stitches. Turn your work around again, to the right side (RS), knit the 5 stitches. Turn the work again to the WS, purl 2 together, purl 1, then purl 2 together. Turn the work to the RS, knit 3 together.

Bound-off edge

This is the edge of an item where you have bound off the stitches, as opposed to the cast-on or beginning edge, or the side edges or selvages.

Brackets

See [ ] on page 25.

Break off

If the instructions say to cut or break the yarn off, leave at least 6–8" (15–20.5 cm) of yarn and WEAVE IN ENDS so that the knitting does not unravel, or leave a longer tail and use this yarn to sew a SEAM.

Button band

A strip of knitting on which you will sew buttons. If the pattern does not indicate which front of a cardigan is to hold the buttons and which should have the buttonholes, traditionally buttons go on the left front for women, and on the right front for men. *See Knitspeak Anatomy on page 190.*

Buttonhole

A buttonhole is an intentional opening in the knitting large enough to allow a button to pass through.

To make a basic buttonhole that is 3 stitches wide:

Row 1: Work to where the buttonhole should be placed (buttonholes should not be right at the edge of a piece, but at least 2 stitches from the edge). **BIND OFF** 3 stitches and work to end of row.

Row 2: On the next row, when you get to the bound-off stitches, use the **BACKWARDS LOOP, KNITTED, OR CABLE CAST-ON METHOD** to cast on 3 stitches and continue knitting.

You can adjust the number of stitches as needed based on the size of your button and the gauge of the knitting.

C

Ca - Circa
About, approximately. Usually found on a yarn label to indicate the approximate length of a given weight of yarn.

Cable
See right.

Cable cast-on
See below.

Cable cast-on

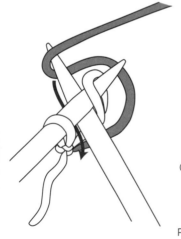

A variation of the knitted cast-on that creates a firm edge, a cable cast-on can also be used to add stitches to existing knitting.

Start with a **SLIP KNOT** on the needle and cast on 1 more stitch using the **KNIT(TED) CAST-ON** method.

Cast on the next and all subsequent stitches by sliding the right-hand needle between the 2 stitches at the end of the left-hand needle, rather than inserting it into a stitch. Pull yarn forward with the needle (as shown) to create a new stitch, and slip it onto the left needle as you would for a Knitted cast-on.

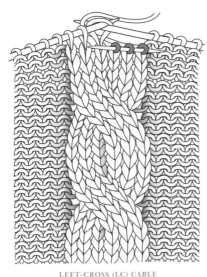

LEFT-CROSS (LC) CABLE

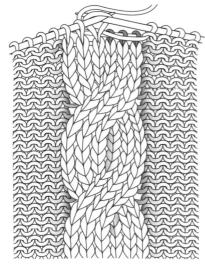

RIGHT-CROSS (RC) CABLE

Cable

A cable is a design feature that creates a ropelike twist in the knitting. It's made by placing a few stitches on hold— usually, with the help of a CABLE NEEDLE—so that the stitches may be worked out of their usual order. If the pattern instructions say to make a 6-stitch cable, place 3 stitches on hold. Hold them in front of the work to create a left cross (LC), or hold them in back of the work to create a right cross (RC). Work the next 3 stitches on the left-hand needle, then work the 3 stitches you had placed on hold, from the cable needle.

Cap

In a sweater with SET-IN SLEEVES, the cap is the portion of the sleeve that covers the wearer's shoulder. It extends from the widest part of the sleeve, through the cap shaping to the top of the sleeve.

CAP

CAP

CAP

Cable needle
See CN.

Carry threads at the back
See Stranding.

Cast off
Another term for BIND OFF.

Cast on
See CO.

Cast-on edge
The edge of the knitting where you cast on stitches at the beginning of your knitted piece. This term serves as a reference point. You might find it used in contrast to NECK EDGE, ARM EDGE, or BOUND-OFF EDGE. For example, a pattern may tell you to work for a certain number of inches, measuring from the cast-on edge.

CC – Contrasting color
Term used for the secondary color in two-color knitting. A pattern will often indicate the colors as main color (MC) and contrasting color (CC) so you can substitute your own color choices for the ones given.

Abbreviations like CC1 and CC2 refer to additional colors.

Ch – Chain
See right.

Chain cast-on
See Knit(ted) cast-on.

Change to double-pointed needles when there are too few stitches to fit on a circular needle.

Patterns call for switching from circular to double-pointed needles when you are decreasing and you get to a point when there are too few stitches to knit comfortably on the circular needle—for example, when shaping the top of a hat.

Make the change at the beginning of a round by dropping one end of the circular needle and using a double-pointed needle to knit the stitches off. You will want to have roughly an equal number of stitches on each DPN.

You may need to slide stitches from one needle to another in order to work decreases; to knit 2 stitches together, both stitches have to be on the same needle.

Ch – Chain
This is the foundation stitch of crochet. A knitting pattern might call for a crocheted chain to be used as a drawstring in a bag, or as a tail on a knitted animal.

To crochet a chain, attach the yarn to a crochet hook with a SLIP KNOT. Wrap working yarn around hook from back to front, catch the working yarn in the hook, and pull it through the loop on the hook. Repeat to desired length, then cut working yarn and run yarn end through last loop in chain and remove hook.

Change to larger/ smaller needles

This instruction indicates that you will need to substitute another size needle for the ones you are using. To change, simple pick up the new needle and begin knitting with it. You do *not* need to transfer all of your stitches from the old needle to the new needle first.

Changing the size of the needle changes the size of the stitches. The lower the size number, the smaller the circumference and the smaller and tighter the stitches. Conversely, the higher the number of the needle, the wider it is, and the larger the stitch.

Some sweater patterns begin with ribbing at the bottom edge that is knit with smaller needles than the body of the piece, giving the garment firm but elastic edges. Changing the size of the needles while keeping the same number of stitches may also be used to subtly shape a garment.

Charts

Charts look like graph paper with symbols to show you what to do, line by line. Almost always you will find a key defining the meaning of each symbol. Chart symbols are not standardized, so you will see variations from one publisher to another. If your pattern does not include a key, see page 28 for the most commonly used symbols.

GUIDELINES FOR READING CHARTS

1. One square represents one stitch. The symbols within the squares tell you how to work the stitches. Refer to the chart's key to understand the meaning of each symbol, or see page 24.

2. Unless otherwise indicated, read the chart from row 1 at the bottom and work up from there.

3. Row numbers at a chart's right edge indicate right-side rows; read them from right to left. Row numbers at a chart's left edge indicate wrong-side rows; read them from left to right. If you are knitting in the round, read from right to left on all rows, as every row is a right-side row.

4. Charts show just the right side of the work. When you are working back and forth, and you turn your knitting so you are facing the wrong side, you have to use the wrong-side interpretation of each symbol. For example, in the chart on page 57, squares with a dot represent stitches to be purled on right-side rows, and knit on wrong-side rows.

5. **REPEATS** (the minimum number of stitches in one pattern sequence) are sometimes marked by bold lines or a bracket outside of the chart. It is often helpful to put **STITCH MARKERS** on your needle to correspond to these divisions. Some patterns move across the knitting in such a way that the sections shift, and for those, you will have to shift the markers as well.

6. If you see a symbol designated on the key as "no stitch," it means that a stitch has been decreased in the current row or on a previous row and no longer exists. The square in the chart is only a placeholder; it doesn't correspond to a stitch on your needles.

Reading a sample chart

The sample chart below shows a pattern of knits and purls worked over a repeat of 5 stitches, plus 1 extra stitch.

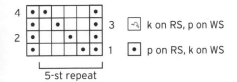

k on RS, p on WS

p on RS, k on WS

5-st repeat

If the directions in the chart were written out for flat knitting, the instructions would look like this:

Row 1 (RS): *P2, k3, repeat from * to last stitch, p1.

Row 2 (WS): K1, *p2, k1, p1, k1, repeat from *.

Row 3: *P1, k2, p1, k1, repeat from * to last stitch, p1.

Row 4: K1, *k1, p3, k1, repeat from *.

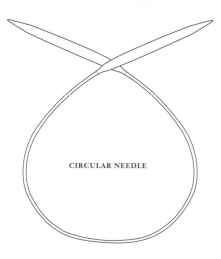

CIRCULAR NEEDLE

Circ – Circular needles

Circular needles consist of two pointed needle tips joined by a flexible plastic or nylon cord. They can be used to knit in the round or to knit back and forth.

Knitting back and forth on circular needles is helpful for an item with a lot of stitches like a shawl or sweater, or when knitting with heavy yarn, as the weight of the knitting stays in the center rather than out at the ends of the needles. In addition, you are less likely to drop and/or lose stitches on circular needles because they don't slip out of the knitting as easily as straight needles.

Circular needles are sold in different lengths (measured from tip to tip) to accommodate different numbers of stitches. A needle that's too short will uncomfortably compress too many stitches in a short space. A needle that's too long will be cumbersome for back-and-forth knitting, and will make knitting in the round impossible: You need enough stitches to extend over the full length of the needle.

		NEEDLE LENGTH			
		16" (40.5 cm)	24" (61 cm)	29" (73.5 cm)	36" (91.5 cm)
GAUGE in stitches per inch	5	80	120	145	180
	6	96	144	174	216
	7	112	168	203	252
	8	128	192	232	288
	9	144	216	261	324

SMALLEST NUMBER OF STITCHES THAT WILL FIT ON A CIRCULAR NEEDLE (when working in the round)

Use the table above to determine what length needle you will need when working in the round. For example, if you're working at a gauge of 6 stitches per inch (2.54 cm) and need to cast on 150 stitches, a 29" (73.5 cm) circular would be too long as it requires a minimum of 174 stitches, but a 24" (61 cm) circular would work as it requires only 144 stitches.

See Join, being careful not to twist for an illustration of joining cast-on stitches into a circle.

Circa
See Ca.

Circular needle
See Circ.

Cm – **Centimeter**

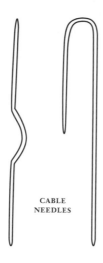

CABLE
NEEDLES

Cn —
Cable needle

A short needle used to hold stitches in the front or back of your work so you can switch the order of the stitches when crossing a cable. You can also use a double-pointed needle or, in a pinch, a toothpick, a pencil, or a chopstick, depending on the size of your stitches.

CO – Cast on

The first step in knitting is to get the loops onto the needle, a process called casting on. Each loop counts as 1 stitch.

At the beginning, a pattern may say simply, "CO 60 sts." There are different ways to cast on, depending on the results you are trying to achieve. If you do not know which one to use, see the table at right. The most common method, the LONG-TAIL CAST-ON, is often a good choice.

Cont – Continue

Continental cast-on
See Long-tail cast-on.

cast-on Tips

1

Cast on using a needle one size larger so that the cast-on edge will not pull in, especially if you are a tight knitter.

2

The cast-on does not constitute a row. The row following the cast-on counts as row 1, the first row of real knitting.

3

If you are making a garment that will get a lot of use and needs to be extra-durable, such as a child's sweater, cast on using yarn from two separate balls. After the cast-on, cut off one strand, leaving a tail to weave in at the end, then continue knitting with the remaining strand.

CHOOSING A CAST-ON	
IF YOU WANT...	THEN USE ...
versatile, elastic	LONG-TAIL CAST-ON
to add stitches to existing knitting	BACKWARDS LOOP, KNITTED, and CABLE CAST-ON
flexible, loose	BACKWARDS LOOP CAST-ON
versatile, easy for beginners	KNITTED CAST-ON
firm, with a chained edge	CABLE CAST-ON
a temporary edge to allow you to add rows, edging, fringe	PROVISIONAL CAST-ON

Note: For instructions on how to work a specific cast-on, look it up in this book by its name.

Continental style
See opposite page.

Continue as established/ Continue in same manner
This means to keep on doing what you are doing, continuing to work the sequence of stitches in the pattern for a certain length or until a new instruction is given.

Contrasting color
See CC.

Crochet hook
See right.

Cut yarn
See Break off.

Crochet hook
A short needle with a crook in one end, used by knitters to pick up dropped stitches and for various cast-ons and edgings.

Continental style

Also known as German style, left-hand
hold, and left-hand carry, Continental
style refers to a style of knitting
in which the knitter holds the working
yarn in the left hand. It is sometimes
called picking to describe the
way the right-hand needle picks
up the yarn.

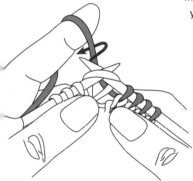

This is in contrast to the
AMERICAN or English style
of holding the yarn
in the right hand, also
known as throwing.

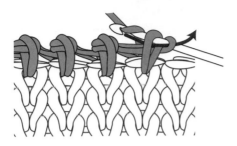

Crab stitch

Also referred to as a reverse single crochet or corded edging, this is a crochet stitch used to create a finished edge with a subtly knotted appearance. Crab stitch is a form of single crochet that is done "backwards," that is, from left to right.

Attach the yarn to the hook with a **SLIP KNOT**. Starting at the left edge of the piece, *insert the crochet hook into the fabric from front to back, draw up a loop, wrap yarn over hook and draw the yarn through both loops on the hook, move one stitch to the right and repeat from *.

Crochet provisional cast-on

Also called crochet-chain cast-on, this is one way of working a PROVISIONAL CAST-ON.

With a crochet hook and contrasting-color WASTE YARN, crochet a CHAIN several links longer than the number of stitches you need to cast on. Bring the waste yarn tail through the last link of the chain to secure it, and tie a knot in the tail so you know at which end of the chain to begin "unzipping" later. With a knitting needle and the yarn you will be using for knitting, starting at the end that is NOT knotted, PICK UP AND KNIT one stitch in each bump at the back of the crochet chain until you have picked up the necessary number of stitches.

Later, when you are ready to use live stitches at the cast-on edge, loosen the waste yarn tail at the knotted end and begin unzipping the chain slowly, catching each stitch on an empty needle.

See WASTE-YARN PROVISIONAL CAST-ON for a provisional cast-on that does not require crochet.

D

Dec – Decrease

Decrease means to reduce the number of stitches. There are many ways to do this, and the method you use depends on the way the piece is shaped and the look you are trying to achieve.

For example, to accentuate the shape of a V-neck, work right-leaning decreases at the left neck edge (on the wearer's left side, not the viewer's left side), and work left-leaning decreases at the opposite neck edge.

CHOOSING A DECREASE	
IF YOU WANT...	THEN USE ...
a general-purpose decrease	K2TOG
a single decrease that slants to the right	K2TOG or P2TOG
a single decrease that slants to the left without twisting stitches	SKP, SSK, or SSP
a single decrease that slants to the left without requiring any slipped stitches	K2TOGTBL or P2TOGTBL
a double decrease that slants to the right	K3TOG or P3TOG
a double decrease that slants to the left	SK2P
a centered double decrease	S2KP

NOTE: For instructions on how to work a decrease, look it up in this book by its abbreviation.

Decreases can be worked as knits or as purls, and as single decreases (reducing two stitches to one) or as double decreases (reducing three stitches to one). Use the table at left to choose among your decrease options.

If you are making a garment piece that will be sewn to another piece later, make your decreases one or two stitches in from the edge so you leave a smooth edge for seaming.

Decrease stitches evenly across row/round

This means that the specified number of decreases must be spaced so they are spread out over the width of the item, as opposed to concentrating all the new stitches in one place.

To determine the intervals at which to decrease, divide the original number of stitches by the number of decreases (if working in the round) or by the number of decreases plus one (if working flat).

For example, if you are working in the round over 80 stitches and need to decrease 10 stitches evenly across the next round, divide 80 by 10 to get 8. Work a decrease every 8 stitches—that is, work 6 stitches, then work a decrease.

If you are working flat, divide 80 by 11 (10 + 1) to get 7.273. Because 7.273 is between 7 and 8, you will work some decreases every 7 stitches, and some every 8 stitches. Multiply 0.273 by 11 to get 3: you will work a decrease every 8 stitches 3 times, then work the remaining 7 decreases every 7 stitches.

Distribute stitches evenly
See Divide stitches evenly on 3 or 4 needles.

Divide stitches evenly on 3 or 4 needles

Also called distribute stitches evenly, this means to distribute all the stitches onto double-pointed needles so that there is roughly an equal number of stitches on each needle. For example, if you were knitting a hat and had cast 60 stitches onto one needle, you would then slide the stitches onto 3 double-pointed needles, putting 20 stitches on each. If you had cast on 65 stitches, you could place 20 stitches on each of two needles and 25 stitches on the third.

....

DK – Double knitting

This term is used in different contexts to mean different things.

On a yarn label or in a pattern's list of yarn requirements, DK refers to a yarn weight that is a little heavier than sportweight, but lighter than worsted-weight. More specifically,

a DK weight is a yarn that will knit at between 5 and 5.5 stitches per inch (20 to 22 stitches per 10 cm).

In a pattern, the term *double knitting* refers to a technique in which two layers of knitting are knitted at the same time to create a double thickness.

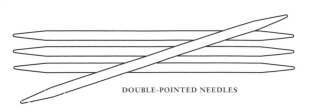

DOUBLE-POINTED NEEDLES

DPN – Double-pointed needles

Straight needles with points at both ends, double-pointed needles are most often used for knitting in the round, especially in cases where there are too few stitches to fit on a circular needle.

They are sold in sets of 4 (3 to hold the work and 1 to knit) or 5 (4 to hold the work and 1 to knit). When available, it's a good idea to buy a set of 5; for some projects you need all 5 and, even if you only need 4, having an extra needle is handy in case one needle gets bent, lost, or broken.

. . . .

Double cast-on
See Long-tail cast-on.

Double ply
See Ply.

Drape

Drape (or hand) refers to the characteristics of a knitted fabric: Does it fold and flow readily, or is it stiff? Fabrics that drape differently are suitable for different purposes. A loose, flowing fabric would be suitable for a shawl. Socks, in contrast, require a firmer fabric for durability.

Drop(ped) shoulder

Dropped shoulder refers to a sweater design in which the body has no special shaping at the armholes to accommodate the sleeves. When such a sweater is worn, the simple straight seam between the body and the top of the sleeve "drops" down on the wearer's upper arm, giving the sweater design its name.

. . . .

Dropped Stitch

This is the term for a stitch that falls off or is taken off a knitting needle unintentionally. When this happens, you need to pick up the dropped stitch or it will unravel downward, creating a ladderlike run in the fabric. For instructions on how to pick up a dropped stitch, see page 208.

In certain stitch patterns, you drop a stitch intentionally to create decorative openwork. The instructions tell you to work a YO or other increase, and several rows later to drop the stitch above the increase; the dropped stitch will then unravel only as far as the increase.

Duplicate stitch
See right.

Duplicate stitch

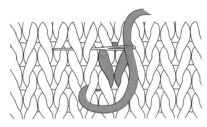

Duplicate stitch is a technique borrowed from embroidery that is worked on top of a knit stitch after the knitting is completed. You can use duplicate stitch to create a motif or pattern in another color on top of the knitting, a technique sometimes called embroidered jacquard. You can also use it to correct mistakes in INTARSIA or STRANDING, to fill in small spots of color, to reinforce weak spots, to cover stains, or to weave in ends.

To duplicate a stitch, bring a threaded yarn needle from back to front in the space below the stitch; this is your "starting point." Trace the path of the stitch with the yarn needle, and return the yarn needle to the back at your starting point. To duplicate a series of stitches, work in horizontal rows, from right to left (for right-handers) or from left to right (for left-handers).

....

Dye lot

A dye lot is a batch of yarn that was put in a dye bath at the same time. Two balls of yarn can appear to be the same shade, but the color won't be an exact match if they don't come from the same dye lot. The dye lot number is on the yarn label—check this number when buying yarn and be sure to buy enough of the same dye lot to complete your project. If you must include a ball from an odd dye lot, consider reserving it for the project's trim, such as its cuffs or neckband, so any slight color difference will appear to be a "design feature." Or blend in the odd ball, making its color difference less noticeable: Alternate between working two rows with the odd ball and two rows with a ball in the correct dye lot. *See How to Read a Yarn Label on page 196.*

E

DESIRED FIT	AMOUNT OF EASE
VERY CLOSE	use actual chest measurement or 1" (2.5 cm) less
CLOSE	add 1-2" (2.5-5 cm) of ease
STANDARD	add 2-4" (5-10 cm) of ease
LOOSE	add 4-6" (10-15 cm) of ease
OVERSIZED	add more than 6" (15 cm) of ease

Ease

In garment sizing, ease refers to the amount of room between your body and the garment. A tight-fitting sweater has little to no ease, meaning there is no gap between the body and the sweater, while a baggy sweater has a lot of room between the body and the sweater, so it has quite a bit of ease.

Ease is added to garments for reasons of fit and style. You need less ease with fine, elastic fabrics than you do with bulky or inelastic fabrics. Add an appropriate amount of ease to your chest measurement before choosing which size of a sweater pattern to knit. Determine an appropriate amount of ease by measuring an existing sweater, or by referring to the table above.

In garment FINISHING, ease refers to the process of subtly gathering one piece of fabric when seaming it to another, smaller piece—for example, when fitting a sleeve CAP into an armhole. Often, it's possible to ease in a seam by dividing each piece into quarters, and matching the quarters as you seam. But to ease in a more dramatic difference in size, use waste yarn to gather the larger piece first—for example, to ease a puff sleeve into an armhole, use waste yarn to baste a loose running stitch around the cap of the puff sleeve, pull on the waste yarn to gather the cap, sew the seam, then remove the waste yarn.

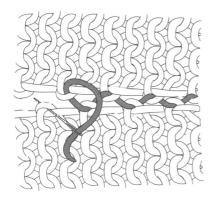

Edge-to-edge seaming

A method of sewing two pieces of knitting together so that the seam will lie flat. It is not a bulky seam, and will look just about invisible, but it is not ideal for a part of a garment that will be under stress such as a shoulder seam.

Bring the selvages (edges) of the fabric next to each other. Bring the yarn through a bump on the edge of first piece, then through a bump on the second piece. Continue in this way, drawing the seam closed every 5 or 6 rows.

Ending on a knit row/ ending on a purl row

If the direction says to end on a knit row, stop after working a knit row. End on a purl row means to stop after working a purl row.

Ending on a right-side row/ ending on a wrong-side row

To end on a right-side row, stop after working a right-side row. To end on a wrong-side row, stop after working a wrong-side row.

English-style hold

See American style.

Entrelac

For this technique, blocks of knitting in one or more colors are worked in different directions to create a textured diamond pattern.

EOR – **Every other row**

ER – **Every row**

EST – **Established**

Even/Work even

To continue working without increasing or decreasing, maintaining the same number of stitches.

Even rows

Refers to all even-numbered rows: Rows 2, 4, 6, 8, and so on.

Evenly spaced

To repeat an instruction at regular intervals—for example, to add fringe at regular intervals along the edge of a scarf. *See Decrease stitches evenly across row/round* or *Increase stitches evenly across row/round.*

Every __ rows

This is a direction to follow a particular instruction on those rows only. For example, if a pattern says to increase 2 stitches every 5th row, you would work 4 rows, then make the increases on the 5th row, work 4 more rows, and make the increases on the 10th row, and so on.

E-wrap cast-on

See Backwards loop cast-on.

F

F&B – Front and back
Front and back loops of a stitch.
See K1f&b.

Fair Isle
Fair Isle is a traditional form of
STRANDING named for one of the
Shetland Islands, off the coast of
Scotland. Classic Fair Isle patterns
use many colors and appear quite
complex, but only two colors
are worked in any one row. It is the
frequent color changes that produce
the complex effect.

The term Fair Isle is sometimes
also used to describe the stranding
technique itself, even if the patterning
is not traditional.

Fasten/Fasten off
To secure the tail end of yarn once
you've bound off your last stitch.
To do so, cut yarn, leaving tail
approximately 6" (15 cm) long
(or longer, if tail will be used for
seaming); pull up on needle,
enlarging last remaining stitch
until the tail pops free.

Felting/Fulling

Felting is when you intentionally shrink wool so that it becomes dense and loses its pliability. Technically, felting is when wool fleece is directly submerged in hot water or shocked by subjecting the fibers to hot and then cold water. If the item is knit first, then shrunk, the correct term for the process is fulling. Most present-day knitting patterns, however, use the term felting to mean shrinking a knitted piece, like a tote bag or slipper socks. In both cases the fabric becomes dense and the stitches all but disappear; the resulting look depends on many factors, including the type of wool and how it was processed initially, the amount of agitation or rolling, the type of water (hard vs. soft), how much (if any) detergent is used, how long the item is left in the water, and the temperature of the water.

Most animal fibers will felt; wool and mohair felt especially well, unless treated to prevent felting (see **SUPERWASH**) while plant and synthetic fibers will not. Both the chemicals the yarn is exposed to during manufacturing and the way the yarn is spun will affect how quickly and to what extent a yarn will felt. Felting is not an exact science. Some yarns tend to felt extremely well; often, people working in yarn stores can direct you to them.

Finishing

A term for the steps necessary to complete a project after the knitting of the main pieces has been completed; these steps might include sewing seams and attaching buttons.

The term finishing is also sometimes used for techniques that you employ *while* knitting that improve the look of the finished item. For example, the technique of working increases and decreases a few stitches in from the selvage (edge) is sometimes described in books as a finishing technique although it is done during the knitting process.

First stitch

The first stitch on the needle is the one nearest the tip.

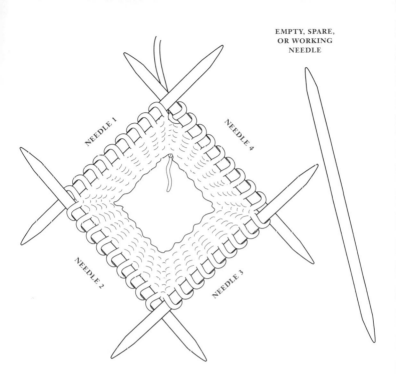

EMPTY, SPARE, OR WORKING NEEDLE

NEEDLE 1

NEEDLE 4

NEEDLE 2

NEEDLE 3

First needle/Needle 1

*Patterns knit in the round will sometimes assign
numbers to the double-pointed needles so that separate
directions can be given for each needle full of stitches.
By convention, the first needle is the one you start with
after joining the knitting into a circle.*

Flat/Knit flat

Knit flat means knitting back and forth rather than in rounds.

Float

When **STRANDING**—that is, when knitting a row with two colors—a float is the strand of yarn of one color that forms on the wrong side of the work as you knit a series of stitches with another color. *See Weave floats.*

Foll – **Following/Follow/Follows**

Foundation row

See Preparation row.

Fringe

See right.

Front

Front can mean multiple things, depending on context.

It can refer to the piece of a project that faces the public, such as the front of a sweater or the front of a pillow.

Or it can refer to the side of your work that faces towards you as you are knitting. For example, "slip purlwise with yarn in front" means to hold the yarn on the side closest to you as you work.

And the "front loop" of a stitch is that part of a stitch on the near side of your needles (in other words, closest to your body). *See illustration on page 122.*

Full/Fulled

See Felting/Fulling.

Full-fashioned

In handknitting, this term generally refers to the practice of designing a garment so that shaping details (usually increases and decreases) are purposely made visible and, thus, become part of the design aesthetic—for example, when shaping is performed several stitches in from the edges of a raglan sleeve or front, causing a very definite, intentional line of stitches to be visible even after seaming.

Fringe

A decorative edge made up of strands of yarn drawn through the edge of a knitted fabric.

To make fringe, begin by wrapping yarn around a piece of cardboard or other object whose width is a bit longer than the length of fringe you want. Cut the threads along one edge. Fold the strands in half, forming a loop. Insert a crochet hook from back to front (or front to back, depending on the look you want) into the fabric's edge and pull the folded loop through the fabric. Bring the ends through the loop and tighten. After you have attached all the fringe, trim the ends of the yarn to the same length with scissors, if desired.

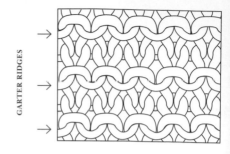

GARTER RIDGES

Garter stitch

The stitch pattern made by knitting every stitch on every row when working back and forth, and by alternating knit and purl rounds when knitting in the round.

Compared to **STOCKINETTE STITCH**, Garter stitch is bulkier, uses more yarn, and has more rows per inch for a given needle size. It's entirely reversible: The surface of both sides is composed of a series of horizontal ridges known as "Garter ridges." Each Garter ridge is created by working two rows (or rounds) of Garter stitch. These ridges allow the fabric to stretch vertically. Unlike Stockinette stitch, Garter stitch does not curl, making it a popular choice for scarves and as an edging for items meant to lie flat.

To create an even, consistent edge in garter stitch, **SLIP** the first stitch of every row as if to purl (bring the yarn to the front, slip the first stitch, then move the yarn to the back to knit).

G

See Gm – Grams.

Gansey/Guernsey

A sweater style that originated in the 19th century in coastal English fishing communities. These hard-wearing garments are traditionally worked tightly in dense, dark yarn with GUSSETS under the arms, DROP(PED) SHOULDERS, and areas of textural stitchwork.

Garter stitch

See left.

Gauge

Gauge (rhymes with sage) is the number of stitches in a horizontal span of knitting, or the number of rows in a vertical span of knitting. Also known as tension, your gauge is determined by how tightly or loosely you knit, and by the size of your needles.

Gauge is usually measured over 4" (10 cm), in a SWATCH. At the beginning of your pattern, you should see a statement of the number of stitches (or stitches and rows) over 4" (10 cm) in a specific stitch pattern. For example, it might say:

> Gauge: 22 sts and 26 rows = 4" (10 cm) in Stockinette stitch

This translates to:
22 stitches worked in Stockinette stitch will yield a piece of fabric 4" (10 cm) wide. You could also say there are 5.5 stitches to the inch (2.5 cm), since 22 divided by 4 is 5.5. Similarly, 26 rows worked in Stockinette stitch will yield 4" (10 cm) of fabric in height, or 6.5 rows will yield 1" (2.5 cm), since 26 divided by 4 is 6.5.

Gauge is very important. Without making a swatch, checking your gauge, and (if necessary) altering your needle size before beginning your project, you have no guarantee that the finished piece will be the desired shape and size. It's always a good idea to buy an extra ball of yarn to ensure that you will have enough for both checking your gauge and completing your project. For more on measuring gauge, see next page.

MEASURING GAUGE AND CHOOSING NEEDLE SIZES

As with many techniques, some knitters have their own favorite ways to measure gauge. You may find another way that suits you, but here is a way to begin:

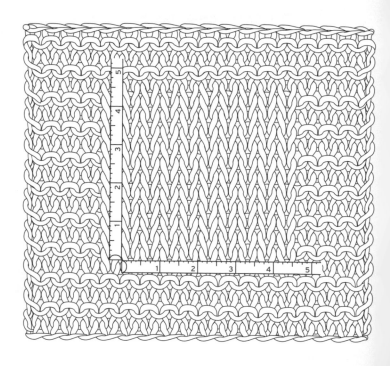

1. Using needles and chosen yarn, cast on 4 stitches and slide a STITCH MARKER onto the needle.

2. CAST ON enough stitches to yield at least 4" (10 cm), or as many as 6" (15 cm) of fabric—for example, if the pattern calls for 20 stitches over 4" (10 cm), cast on 20 to 30 stitches. If the pattern specifies gauge over a STITCH PATTERN other than STOCKINETTE STITCH, cast on an appropriate number of stitches for that stitch pattern—for example, if the stitch pattern has a MULTIPLE of 5 stitches plus 3, you could cast on 23 or 28 stitches.

3. Place another marker and cast on 4 more stitches so you have 4 extra stitches on each side of center stitches.

4. Work 4 rows, knitting all the stitches in each row. This creates a GARTER STITCH border that will help the fabric to lie flat and make it easier to measure gauge.

5. On the following rows, knit the first 4 stitches (before the first marker) and the last 4 stitches (after the second marker) to continue the Garter stitch border. Work the stitches in the middle using the stitch pattern named by the pattern's gauge specification. Continue for at least 4" (10 cm).

6. Work 4 more rows in Garter stitch to complete the border, and bind off all the stitches loosely.

7. Wash, BLOCK, and dry the piece as you intend to wash, block, and dry the item you are making. Check the symbols on the yarn label for washing instructions. See page 201 for symbol key.

8. Measuring only stitches worked in the required stitch pattern, inside Garter stitch border, count the number of stitches and rows in 4" (10 cm). If the pattern tells you to measure the gauge "slightly stretched" (as in ribbing, for example), pin or hold the swatch to approximate how stretched it will be in use. Measure in a few places and average the results to get an accurate overall measurement.

If you come up with too few or too many stitches, knit a new swatch, using a different needle size. Use a larger needle to create larger stitches and produce a gauge with fewer stitches per inch. Use a smaller needle to create smaller stitches and produce a gauge with more stitches per inch. Repeat steps 1 through 8 until you determine the needle size that produces a fabric of the correct gauge for your pattern.

Warning! If your gauge is only off by a half-stitch per inch, you may be tempted to stop swatching and start knitting. But consider the implications: A small difference in gauge can make a big difference in fit. For example, to knit a 20" (51 cm) hat in bulky yarn, a pattern might tell you to match a gauge of 3 stitches per inch (12 stitches per 4" [10 cm]), and to cast on 60 stitches. Getting a gauge of 2.5 stitches per inch (10 stitches per 4" [10 cm]), however, would yield a 24" (61 cm) hat, which would create quite a different look and fit from the one intended by the pattern.

(continued on next page)

9. When you've achieved the correct gauge for your pattern, staple the yarn label and a piece of yarn to an index card. Staple or tie the swatch to it. Write on the card the needle size used to knit the swatch, and the number of stitches and rows per inch.

Note: If the project is knit in the round, to be precise, you should knit the gauge swatch in the round. For small projects, such as a hat, some people knit the first few inches, measure gauge, and restart if necessary. Similarly, for sweaters, some knitters start with a sleeve, or buy extra yarn and knit a matching hat as an in-the-round gauge swatch. Be aware, however, that if you don't wash and block your knitting before measuring gauge, there is a chance that it will not be accurate.

Gm – **Grams**

Grams, the metric measuring unit for weight, is used on yarn labels to indicate the weight of the yarn in the ball. There are 28.3 grams in an ounce. For help in converting between grams and ounces, *see page 219.*

Most labels include both the weight and the length of the yarn. The length in yards or meters is more useful than the weight for determining how many balls are required to complete a particular pattern. For tips on determining how many balls to buy for a project, *see page 204.*

Grafting
See Kitchener stitch.

Gram
See Gm - Grams.

Graph
Also called Chart. *See page 54.*

Gusset
A gusset is a triangular or diamond-shaped piece of fabric knit into a garment to improve its fit. The most common places for gussets are where the thumb joins the hand in a mitten or glove, where the heel joins the foot in a sock, and under the arms of sweaters. *See Knitspeak Anatomy on page 190.*

H

Hand
See Drape.

Holder
See Stitch holder.

Heel flap

Some socks are made with heel flaps, rectangular fabric pieces that cover the heel back. They are knit back and forth over roughly half the sock's stitches, then stitches are picked up along its selvages and the remainder of sock is completed in the round. *See page 191.*

I

I-cord
See below.

In – **Inch**

In patt – **In pattern**

This means to continue to work the stitch pattern that has been established or explained previously. The instructions may tell you to work knit 2, purl 2 ribbing, then say to continue in pattern for 2" (5 cm). That means that after the initial row, you would work in ribbing until the pieces measure 2" (5 cm).

....

I-cord

A knitted cord most commonly used as a drawstring or tie.

To make a 3-stitch I-cord, cast 3 stitches onto a double-pointed needle (DPN). With a second DPN knit the 3 stitches. Do not turn your work. Slide the stitches back to the right-hand end of the needle without turning and knit them again, pulling the working yarn snugly across the back. Repeat until you have the desired length cord.

In same manner
See Continue as established.

Inc – **Increase**

This means to add new stitches to a row or round; there are many ways to do this. In cases where a pattern does not specify the type of increase to use, many knitters choose to knit into the front and back of the next stitch (abbreviated as **K1F&B** and also called a **BAR INCREASE**). Use the table below to choose among increase options.

Note that k1f&b and p1f&b are worked *in* a stitch, turning a single stitch into two, while the other increases are worked *between* two stitches. If you are making a garment piece that will be sewn to another piece later, it's often helpful to make your increases one or two stitches in from the edge so you leave a smooth edge for seaming.

CHOOSING AN INCREASE	
IF YOU WANT...	THEN USE...
a short, decorative, horizontal bar	K1F&B
an increase with 2 purl bumps	P1F&B
a small decorative hole	YO
an increase with a twist to the right	M1R
an increase with a twist to the left	M1L
an increase that slants to the right of a stitch	RLI
an increase that slants to the left of a stitch	LLI
a nearly invisible increase	KRB

NOTE: For instructions on how to work each increase, look it up in this book by its abbreviation.

Increase stitches evenly across row/round

This means that the specified number of increases must be spaced so they are spread out over the width of the item, as opposed to concentrating all the new stitches in one place.

To determine the intervals at which to add new stitches, divide the original number of stitches by the number of increases (if working in the round) or by the number of increases plus one (if working flat).

For example, if you are working in the round over 80 stitches and need to increase 10 stitches evenly across the next round, divide 80 by 10 to get 8. Work an increase after every 8th stitch.

If you are working flat, divide 80 by 11 (10 + 1) to get 7.273. Because 7.273 is between 7 and 8, you will work some increases every 7 stitches, and some every 8 stitches. Multiply 0.273 by 11 to get 3: you will work an increase after every 8th stitch 3 times, then work the remaining 7 increases after every 7th stitch.

Intarsia
See right.

Invisible seam
See Mattress stitch.

Intarsia

Intarsia, also known as picture knitting, is a technique where blocks of color are worked independently, each color having its own short length of yarn (often wound onto a BOBBIN*) in order to create a picture, such as a heart or star. The yarns are not carried along on the wrong side of the work as in* STRANDING *but are twisted at each color change, with the new color coming over the old, to make a smooth join without leaving any holes.*

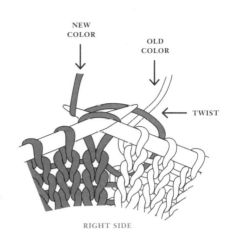

RIGHT SIDE

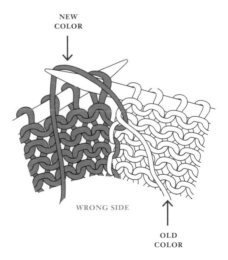

WRONG SIDE

J

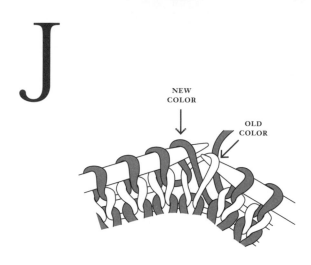

NEW COLOR

OLD COLOR

....

Jog/Jogless

The meeting point of a round of knitting on circular or double-pointed needles creates a stair step, called a jog. This is often quite apparent in stripes or other multicolored patterns. To make it less obvious, position this meeting point at the back of a piece or at some other point where it is not likely to be noticed.

One way to minimize the jog in stripes or multicolored knitting is to work one full round in the new color, then knit the first stitch of the next round together with the stitch from the row below, as follows:

Insert the tip of the right needle into the old-color stitch below the first stitch on the left needle (as shown in the illustration at left), and knit it together with the new-color stitch on the left needle.

Note that jogs can also occur in one-color textured knitting. Sometimes you can avoid this by selecting carefully where in the patterning you want each round to start (for example, next to a column of plain knit stitches) or by adjusting the stitch count (for example, working **SEED STITCH** in the round over an odd number of stitches will assure that your knits and purls always occur in the correct place).

Join another ball of yarn/ Join a new color

See Attach a new ball of yarn.

Join, being careful not to twist

This is a direction found in patterns that are worked in the round, using either double-pointed or circular needles. After casting on, you will join the ends of the knitting into a circle, and do so without twisting the line of stitches.

On double-pointed needles, **DIVIDE STITCHES EVENLY ON 3 OR 4 NEEDLES**, and arrange the needles with beginning and end stitches at the top.

For circulars, move the stitches around until the ends meet at the tips of the needles.

Line up the knotted side of the cast-on stitches so that you can see an unbroken line all the way around, that is, you have "knots" on the inside and loops on the outside. If, after a few rounds of knitting, you notice there is a twist in your work, you must rip out the piece and cast on again, so be careful at this point to keep the stitches aligned.

There are several ways to join the cast-on stitches.

The simplest way to join (shown at right) is to begin by working the first stitch on the left-hand needle, using the yarn coming from the last stitch on the right-hand needle. Then when you have worked all the stitches and are back to the place where you joined the knitting, you have made one round. Slide a **STITCH MARKER** here so you can tell where the rounds begin.

Another method is to cast on one extra stitch. To join, slide the new stitch from the right-hand needle onto the left needle, and then work that stitch together with the next stitch as if they were one.

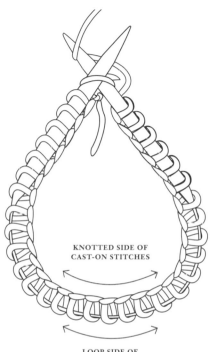

**KNOTTED SIDE OF
CAST-ON STITCHES**

**LOOP SIDE OF
CAST-ON STITCHES**

A third variation is to cast on one extra stitch, work the first stitch of the new round, and slip the second stitch on the right-hand needle (the extra cast-on stitch) over that stitch.

Some people find it easier to work one or two rows in flat, back-and-forth knitting before making the join. This way it is easier to make sure the knitting does not twist. If you do this, leave a long tail; later, use it to sew closed the slit at the beginning of rounds.

(*See Divide stitches evenly on 3 or 4 needles* to see how joined stitches look on double-pointed needles.)

K

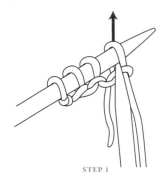

STEP 1

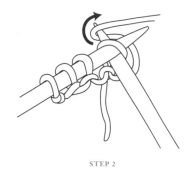

STEP 2

K- Knit

K is the abbreviation for the knit stitch. The word knit can refer to the general activity of knitting or to the making of a knit stitch; you will be able to determine from context which meaning is being used. Usually if the abbreviation K is used, it refers to making a knit stitch.

step 1

To make a knit stitch, bring the yarn between the needle tips to the back of your work, and slide the right-hand needle up underneath the front leg of the first stitch on the left-hand needle and away from you.

step 2

Bring the yarn around the right-hand needle as shown in the illustration above.

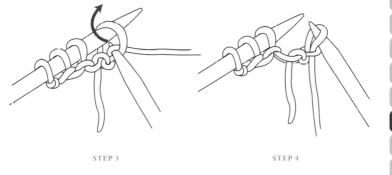

STEP 3   STEP 4

step 3

Keeping the yarn on the right-hand needle, bring the needle forward under the front leg of the old stitch in order to pull the yarn through and create a new stitch.

step 4

Use your right-hand needle to lift the old loop off the left needle. The new loop on the right-hand needle counts as one stitch.

Some people find it helpful to use a rhyme to remember the steps. For example:

In through the front door,
Dance around the back,
Out through the window,
And off jumps Jack.

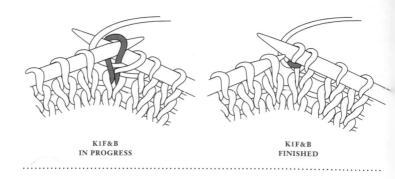

K1F&B
IN PROGRESS

K1F&B
FINISHED

K1f&b –
Knit 1 front and back

Knit 1 front and back is a common way to add a stitch.
This is a visible increase—a horizontal bar is created when
you make it. Sometimes known as a bar increase, it can
be used as a design element—for example, to emphasize
the shaping of a garment.

Begin by knitting the stitch as usual, but before pulling the
original stitch off the left-hand needle, guide the right-hand
needle under the back loop of the stitch (as shown in the
illustration on the left above). Bring the yarn around the needle
as when knitting normally, pull a new loop forward, and slip
the original stitch and the new stitch off the left-hand needle
(as you would a standard knit stitch).

K1, p1 rib/K2, p2 rib
See Rib/Ribbing.

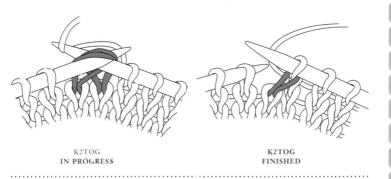

K2TOG
IN PROGRESS

K2TOG
FINISHED

K2tog –
Knit 2 together

This is a common way to decrease, that is, to take away a stitch. If the pattern does not indicate which decrease to use, you are usually safe with the k2tog. The resulting stitch will slant to the right.

Slide your right-hand needle up and under the front leg of the *second* stitch on the left-hand needle and then under the front leg of the first stitch (entering both stitches just as you would a standard knit stitch, as shown). Then knit both together as if they were one stitch.

The mirror-image counterparts to k2tog are SKP and SSK, two left-leaning decreases.

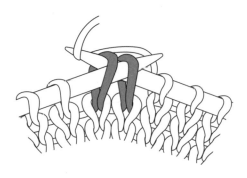

K2togtbl –
Knit 2 together through back loops

This decrease is similar to K2TOG. The only difference is that you insert the right-hand needle into the back loops of the stitches rather than the front loops—that is, slide your right-hand needle through the back loops of the next two stitches on the left-hand needle, and knit them together as if they were one stitch.

A k2togtbl decrease slants to the left. It is quick and easy to work; however, because it twists the stitches, it is not a perfect mirror-image of a k2tog. For a perfect mirror-image of k2tog, see Ssk.

K3tog – **Knit 3 together**

K3tog is a decrease that reduces three stitches to one. Like K2TOG, it leans to the right.

To work a k3tog, insert the right-hand needle up into the first three stitches on the left needle, and knit them together as one.

Kb

This abbreviation is used to refer to multiple techniques. You will be able to determine which technique to use from context, or by reading your pattern's abbreviations list.

Kb most often signifies knit into the back of the stitch, described under KTBL. This produces a twisted stitch, but does not add a new stitch to the row.

Kb is also sometimes used instead of KRB to mean knit in the row below to create an increase. An alternate form of knitting in the row below is used to work a JOGLESS JOG, or is used to create an elongated stitch for decorative effect in certain stitch patterns.

Kb can also mean to knit with a bead. Refer to your pattern's instructions for more information on knitting with beads.

Keep/Maintain pattern as established
See Maintain patt.

Kfb
See K1f&b.

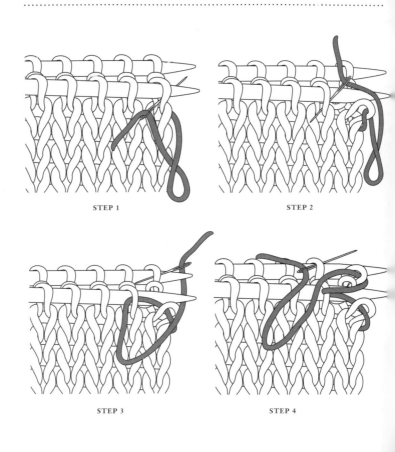

STEP 1

STEP 2

STEP 3

STEP 4

Kitchener stitch

The Kitchener stitch is a method of grafting two pieces of knitting together so the join looks like another row of knitting.

To start, break off the yarn, leaving a tail four times as long as the join. Thread tail onto a yarn needle.

step 1

Holding needles parallel, wrong sides together, guide the tip of yarn needle through the first stitch on the front needle as if you were going to knit, pull the yarn through the loop, and slide that same loop off the needle.

step 2

Bring the yarn needle through the next stitch on the front needle as if to purl, pull the yarn through, and leave the stitch on the needle.

step 3

Bring the yarn around the tips of the needles, and guide it through the first stitch on the back needle as if to purl, bring the yarn through, and slide the stitch off the needle.

step 4

Bring the needle through the next stitch on the back needle as if to knit, pull the yarn through, and leave it on the needle.

Repeat these 4 steps across the row until one stitch remains. Draw the thread through the last stitch, and **WEAVE IN ENDS**. Here's an abbreviated version of the process:

Front knit off, front purl on,
Back purl off, back knit on.

Knit
See K – Knit.

Knit across
See Acr – Across.

Knit(ted) cast-on
See right.

Knit into front and back of stitch
See K1f&b.

Knit plain
Knit plain can mean a couple things. Most of the time it means to continue without increasing or decreasing, as in **WORK EVEN**. In some older patterns, it means to create knit stitches only, no purl stitches—that is, to create **GARTER STITCH** when working flat. To determine which meaning applies, study the photograph that accompanies your pattern.

Knit up stitches
British term for pick up stitches; *see PU.*

Knitwise
See As if to knit.

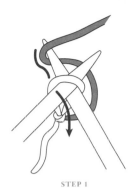

STEP 1   STEP 2

Knit(ted) cast-on

Also called a chain cast-on, this is a method of creating
loops on the needle so you can start knitting. It can
also be used to add stitches to existing knitting—for
example, when adding new stitches for a buttonhole
or a mitten thumb.

Make a **SLIP KNOT** and place it on one needle; hold this
needle in your left hand. With an empty needle, knit into this
stitch (see Step 1), but instead of slipping this stitch off
the left-hand needle, pull the right-hand needle toward you
to loosen up the newly-created stitch, and slip it onto
the left-hand needle by following the course of the red arrow
given in step 2 above—the left-hand needle goes up from
underneath the new stitch so that the side of the loop that
is closest to you becomes the back leg of the new stitch.

Continue adding stitches until you have the required number.

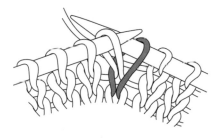

....

Krb –
Knit in the row below

This form of LIFTED INCREASE creates a nearly invisible increase.

Guide the right-hand needle from back to front into the stitch below the next stitch on the left-hand needle, and under the left-hand needle. Wrap the yarn around the right-hand needle as you would for an ordinary knit stitch, and pull the yarn forward through the old stitch to create a new stitch. You have done this correctly if you find this twists the old stitch. You are now ready to work the next stitch on the left-hand needle.

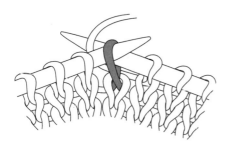

Ktbl –
Knit through back loop

Knitting through the back of the loop causes the knit
stitch to be twisted and tighter than knitting through the
front of the loop (as in conventional knitting). A pattern
might indicate to knit through the back loop in order to
tighten one stitch at the end of a buttonhole or at the heel
GUSSET of a sock. In some traditions, all the knit stitches
of a garment might be knit through their back loops
for decorative effect.

Kw/Kwise – Knitwise
See As if to knit.

L

Ladder stitch
See Mattress stitch.

L – Left

This may refer to the left-hand needle, usually the one that holds the stitches to be knit. It can also refer to the left side of a garment—that is, the side that would be on your left when you wear the garment.

LC – Left cross

This is a cable crossing that twists up and to the left. *See Cable.*

Left
See L - Left.

Left-hand hold

Also known as **CONTINENTAL STYLE** or picking, this term refers not to being left-handed, but to the hand that holds the yarn that comes from the ball. As distinguished from **AMERICAN STYLE** or English hold.

LH – Left hand

LHN – Left-hand needle

Lifted increase

Lifted increases are inconspicuous increases worked by lifting a stitch from the row below. See RLI for a lifted increase that slants to the right of an existing stitch, or LLI for one that slants to the left. If the pattern does not say if a lifted increase should be to the left or right, use a right lifted increase. *See also Krb* for an increase similar to RLI that is nearly invisible.

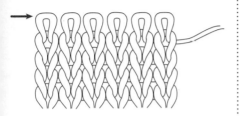

Live stitches

Live stitches are stitches that are not bound off. If you slip your needles out of your work, you will see the live stitches as a row of loops. Live stitches will easily unravel if you pull the WORKING YARN—*unless they are bound off, or are put on a* STITCH HOLDER, WASTE YARN, *or a spare needle.*

LLI
See right

Long-tail cast-on
See page 112

Lp – Loop
In knitting, each circle of yarn around the needle is a loop, and is equal to one stitch.

LLI –
Left lifted increase

This inconspicuous increase results in a stitch that slants to the left of an existing stitch.

To make a left lifted increase, insert tip of left needle from front to back under the left leg of the stitch *two* rows below the first stitch on the right needle, lifting this loop onto the left needle. Knit into this loop to create a new stitch. You are doing this correctly if the new stitch is not twisted. *See Mounted.*

The mirror-image counterpart to LLI is RLI.

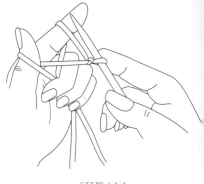

STEPS 1 & 2

Long-tail cast-on

Also called slingshot method, two-tailed cast-on, double cast-on, or continental cast-on, the long-tail cast-on creates an edge that is elastic yet sturdy. To make a long-tail cast-on:

step 1
Measure out a length of yarn about four times the width of the finished piece—for a sweater front 20" (51 cm) wide, leave an 80" (203 cm) tail. At that point, make a **SLIP KNOT** and slide it onto one of the needles, making the loop snug but not tight; this slip knot counts as your first stitch. Hold the needle in your right hand, and hold the slip knot steady with the thumb or index finger of your right hand.

step 2
Wrap the working yarn around your left index finger and the tail yarn over your left thumb about 3" (7.5 cm) from the needle. Hold both yarn ends with the last 3 fingers of your left hand. Pull back with the needle in your right hand. This is the "slingshot" position.

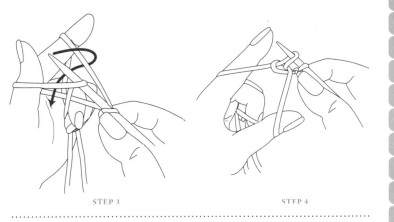

STEP 3   STEP 4

step 3

Guide the tip of the needle up along your thumb, under the yarn in front of your thumb, over and behind the yarn on your index finger, and down through the loop on your thumb.

step 4

Extricate your thumb from its loop, and use it to tug on the yarn tail and tighten the new stitch on the needle.

Repeat steps 2–4 until you have the number of stitches called for in the pattern.

As you are casting on, the loops may twist around the needle. As you prepare to work the first row, line up the knots on one side, loops on the other.

NOTE: Here's a nifty trick that eliminates the knot at the base of the first stitch cast on: Instead of beginning by placing a slip knot on the needle, just measure out the yarn tail and drape it over the needle. Hold this bit of yarn steady with the thumb or index finger of your right hand, then continue with steps 2–4.

M

M

"M" can stand for marker or meter.

A marker is a device that helps you keep track of your knitting. *See Stitch Marker* and *Row Marker.* For tips on using markers to keep track of what you are doing in a pattern, *see page 20.*

A meter is a metric measure of length. *See the conversion table on page 219.*

M1 – Make 1

A Make 1 is an increase worked into the **BAR** (that is, the horizontal strand of yarn) between two stitches. Different kinds of Make 1 exist: **M1L** has a left twist, and **M1R** has a right twist. If your pattern doesn't tell you which kind of Make 1 to use, then use M1L.

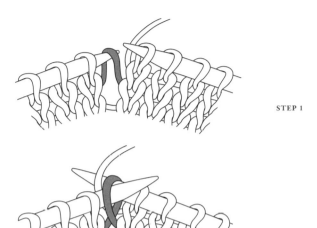

STEP 1

STEP 2

M1L – Make 1 left

Make 1 left adds a new stitch with a left-slanting appearance.

Move the **WORKING YARN** to the back, then move your needles slightly apart and insert the tip of the left-hand needle from the front of the work to the back, under the horizontal yarn **BAR** that runs between the two needles (see Step 1 illustration). Knit into the back leg of this loop (see Step 2 illustration). You know you're creating the Make 1 left correctly if the resulting stitch is twisted to the left.

The mirror-image counterpart of M1L is M1R.

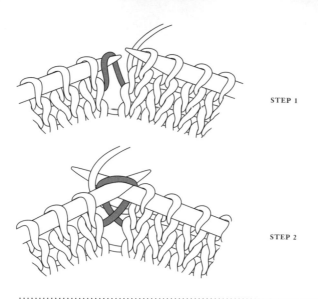

STEP 1

STEP 2

M1R – Make 1 right

Make 1 right adds a new stitch with a right-slanting appearance.

Move the **WORKING YARN** to the back, then move your needles slightly apart and insert the tip of the left-hand needle from the back of the work to the front, under the horizontal yarn **BAR** that runs between the two needles (see Step 1 illustration). Knit into the front leg of this loop (see Step 2 illustration). You know you're creating the Make 1 right correctly if the resulting stitch is twisted to the right.

The mirror-image counterpart of M1R **is M1L.**

Maintain patt – **Maintain pattern as established**

This phrase means to continue working in a stitch pattern as given, even if there are increases and decreases at the edges or—if working vertical waist darts—in the center of the fabric. Rather than writing out the same stitch pattern instructions over and over again, the pattern writer gives them once and tells you to continue, usually for a given number of inches.

Make a stitch

British term for INCREASE.

Making up

This is another term that means FINISHING the item, usually sewing the pieces together. *See Seam/Seaming.*

Mark center stitches

A pattern might tell you to mark the center stitches of an item—for example, of a neckline or a heel flap—so that you can make the shaping symmetrical on each side. To mark the center stitches, divide the total number of stitches in half, and place a STITCH MARKER in the space between the 2 center stitches. Or, if the stitch count is odd, place a marker *in* the center stitch—for example, if a heel flap contains 17 stitches, place a marker in the 9th stitch.

Marker

See M.

Materials

The materials section of a pattern usually lists the yarn brand and type, the amount of yarn required, and the needle size needed to knit the pattern. Other tools or small items that might be required for knitting or finishing may be listed here, or under the NOTIONS section of the pattern.

Mattress stitch

Also called ladder stitch or invisible seaming, this is a way to sew almost invisible seams, with little bulk on the inside.

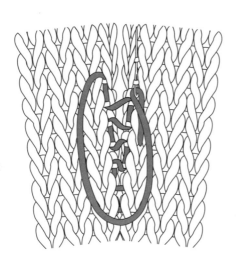

Begin with the right (or public) sides of the two pieces facing you, next to each other. Use the figure-eight start described in **SEAMING**.

Pull the edge of the knitting out until you see a ladder-like series of bars going up between the first and second whole stitches of each row. Slide the yarn needle under two of these horizontal bars, then cross to the other piece and do the same. Continue, aiming the needle down into the point where you last came up on that piece, and going under two horizontal bars. Every few stitches, pull the yarn snug to close up the edges. If you are doing this correctly, when you pull the seam closed the columns of stitches will line up and the seam will be practically invisible.

MC – Main color

When a pattern uses more than one color, it will often label them as main color (MC) and contrasting color (CC) so that you can substitute your own color choices for the ones given. The main color is the one that is used for the background. Each additional contrasting color will be labeled as CC1, CC2, and so on.

Meas – Measuring/Measures

To measure the length of your knitting, place the work flat on a table (or on a hanger if you think the fabric might stretch in use) and measure from the cast-on edge to the edge of the needle, not including the needle itself. If a pattern wants you to use a different method, such as measuring from the top of a piece's ribbing, it will say so in the directions.

To measure the length of a piece with a curved or slanted edge—for example, the length of a neck opening or an armhole—lay a ruler or other straight edge horizontally at the first row of bound-off or decreased stitches, and measure up from the straight edge.

If a pattern says to measure a swatch "slightly stretched," pull each end of the fabric slightly to mimic how the fabric will look (and how much it will be stretched) in the final piece. Pin the stretched swatch and measure it.

To measure a person so you can compare those measurements to the sizes given in a pattern, *see page 120.*

Miss a stitch

British term for SLIP a stitch.

Mm – Millimeter

Knitting needles are usually labeled in both US and metric sizes. A 5 mm needle is 5 millimeters in diameter and equivalent to a size US 8. US sizes do not refer to the dimensions of the needle, but are based on an old wire-measuring system. *See the conversion table on page 219.*

CONVENTIONS FOR MEASURING

Chest/bust Measure around the widest part of the chest, the fullest part of the bust. Do not draw the tape too tightly.

Center back neck to end of sleeve cuff at wrist With the arm slightly bent, measure from the back base of the neck across the shoulder, around the bend of the elbow to the wrist.

Back, from neck to waist Measure from the prominent bone at the base of the neck to the waistline.

Cross back at shoulder blades Measure from shoulder "point" (the tip of the pointed bone at the outside edge of the shoulder) to shoulder point.

Sleeve With the arm slightly bent, measure from the armpit to the cuff edge at the wrist.

Head circumferences With the tape measure across the widest part of the forehead, measure around the full circumference of the head. Pull the tape taut over hair to get the most accurate results.

Adapted from the Yarn Standards of the Craft Yarn Council of America

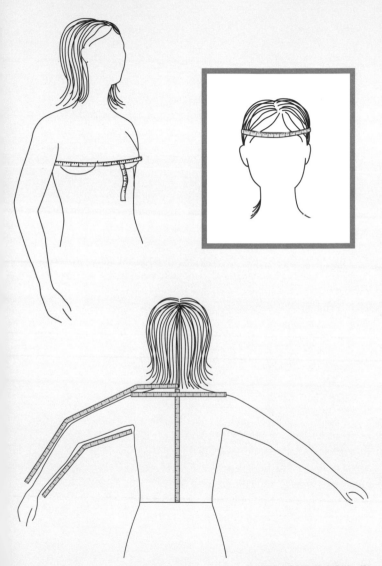

CONVENTIONALLY MOUNTED

RIGHT (LEADING) LEG IN FRONT

UNCONVENTIONALLY MOUNTED

RIGHT (LEADING) LEG IN BACK

. . . .

Mounted

Mounted refers to the way the stitches sit on the needle. A pattern might tell you to make sure your stitches are mounted correctly if you have had to take the stitches off and put them back on the needle, such as moving stitches back and forth from a stitch holder.

By convention in standard American or Western-style knitting, a stitch is mounted "correctly" if the right leg of the stitch sits in front of the needle. Stated another way, the leading leg of the stitch—the leg closest to the tip of the left needle—should be in front of the needle.

Most publications (including this book) give instructions that work as intended only if your stitches are mounted conventionally. Knitting through the front leg of an unconventionally-mounted stitch, for example, results in a twisted stitch. If you discover some stitches are mounted unconventionally, turn them around into conventional mounting before working them.

Motif

A motif is a single element of a design, like a flower or a star, or a series of elements that recur throughout a design.

Mounted

See left.

Multiple/Multiple of

A multiple is the smallest number of stitches required to complete a stitch pattern sequence. For example, K2, P2 Rib is made up of 2 knit stitches and 2 purl stitches, thus it is 4 stitches wide and has a multiple of 4 stitches. These 4 stitches are repeated in sequence multiple times across each row.

Some patterns require extra stitches at one or both edges to "balance" the pattern visually. These extra stitches are worked only once in every row. For example, a Wide Rib pattern with 5 knit stitches and 2 purl stitches might be described as having a multiple of 7 stitches plus 5:

Row 1 (RS): *K5, p2, repeat from * to last 5 sts, k5.
Row 2 (WS): P5, *k2, p5, repeat from *.

This way, the 5 extra stitches at one end ensure that the knit ribs are centered on each knitted piece.

N

Narrow

In old patterns, this is a verb that means to knit 2 stitches together. *See K2tog.*

Neckband

The neckband is the section of a sweater that makes a finished edge around the neck. *See Knitspeak Anatomy on page 190.*

In some patterns the word neckband is used interchangeably with the word collar, though technically a neckband lies flat while a collar stands up and/or folds over.

Neck edge

The edge of the garment closest to the neck; usually in contrast to the arm or shoulder edge. *See page 31.*

Needle gauge

See right.

Needle 1

See First needle.

Needle gauge

A flat tool with a range of graduated holes used to measure the size of knitting needles.

This tool often includes a gauge for crochet hooks and a window for measuring GAUGE on a piece of knitted fabric. To test needle size, slip the needle into the holes. The smallest one that allows the entire needle to pass through easily is your needle size. Often sizes are listed in both the metric and U.S. sizes. This tool comes in handy when the needle size is not marked on the needles themselves. Note that needle size sometimes varies slightly from manufacturer to manufacturer.

No. – **Number**

No stitch

If you see a symbol on a chart, designated on the chart key as "no stitch," it means that a stitch has been decreased in the current row or in a previous row and no longer exists. The square in the chart is only a place holder; it doesn't correspond to a stitch on your needles.

Notions

Patterns use this word to describe any small items you will need in addition to yarn and needles, such as STITCH MARKERS, safety pins, CABLE NEEDLES, and YARN NEEDLES. Notions may also include things needed to finish the item for use, such as linings, zippers, buttons, and more.

O

Odd rows

Refers to all odd-numbered rows: Rows 1, 3, 5, 7, and so on.

Or size to obtain gauge

Patterns often specify a suggested needle size followed by the phrase "or size to obtain gauge." This means you should substitute needles of a different size if necessary to match the pattern's required gauge. *See Gauge* for more information.

Over

See Work over ___ stitches.

Oz – Ounce

Ounces are used to measure the weight of a ball or skein of yarn. For help in converting between ounces and grams, *see page 219.*

Most labels include both the weight and the length of the yarn. The length in yards or meters is more accurate than the weight for determining how many balls are required to complete a particular pattern. For tips on determining how much yarn you need for a project, *see pages 192 and 204.*

P

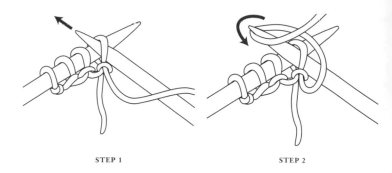

STEP 1   STEP 2

P — Purl

A purl stitch is the converse of
a knit stitch—that is, working a purl
stitch on one side of the fabric is
the same as working a knit stitch
on the other side. Specifically,
working a purl stitch creates a
bump at the base of the needle on
the side facing the knitter, and
a V on the other side. Alternating
rows of knit and purl creates a
fabric called STOCKINETTE STITCH.

step 1
To make a purl stitch, bring the
yarn between the needle tips
to the front of your work, and insert
the right-hand needle under the
front leg of the stitch nearest the
tip the left needle.

step 2
Bring the yarn over the top of
and around the tip of the
right-hand needle.

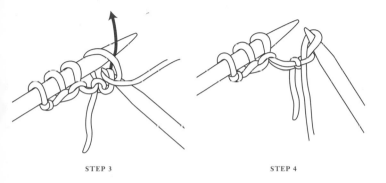

STEP 3 STEP 4

step 3
Keeping the yarn on the right-hand needle, bring the needle back under the front leg of the old stitch in order to pull the yarn backward and create a new stitch.

step 4
Use your right-hand needle to tug the old loop off the left needle. The new loop on the right-hand needle counts as 1 stitch.

P2tog –
Purl 2 together

This is a method of reducing the number of stitches on the needles. It produces a purl stitch that slants to the right.

To purl 2 together, insert the right-hand needle from right to left into the next two stitches on the left-hand needle, and purl them together as if they were one stitch.

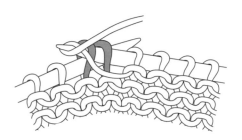

P2tog is the converse of **K2TOG**—that is, working p2tog on one side of the fabric is the same as working k2tog on the other side. The mirror-image counterpart to p2tog is **SSP**.

. . . .

P1f&b - **Purl 1 front and back**
Purl 1 front and back is an increase that results in two small purl bumps. As such, it blends seamlessly into stitch patterns composed primarily of purl stitches—for example, **REVERSE STOCKINETTE STITCH.**

To do this, purl into the front leg of the next stitch as usual, leaving that stitch on the left needle. Purl into its back leg, then drop it off the left needle.

See Ptbl for an illustration of purling into the back leg of a stitch. Or, see right for an illustration of purling through the back of two stitches at the same time.

P2togtbl –
Purl 2 together through back loops

Like P2TOG, P2togtbl reduces two stitches to one.
It produces a purl stitch that slants to the left.

To do this, insert the right-hand needle into the
next two stitches on the left-hand needle from behind
the back leg of the second stitch, and purl them
together as if they were one stitch.

Although p2togtbl slants to the left, it is not a perfect
mirror-image of a p2tog because it twists its stitches.
For a perfect mirror-image of a p2tog, *see Ssp.*

P2togtbl is the converse of **K2TOGTBL**—that is, working
p2togtbl on one side of the fabric is the same as
working k2togtbl on the other side.

P3tog – **Purl 3 together**

P3tog is a double decrease that reduces three stitches to one. Like **P2TOG**, it leans to the right.

To work a p3tog, insert the right-hand needle down into the first three stitches on the left needle, and purl them together as if they were one stitch.

P3tog is the converse of **K3TOG**—that is, working p3tog on one side of the fabric is the same as working k3tog on the other side.

Parentheses
See ( ) on page 26.

Pat/Patt – **Pattern**

This is an abbreviation for the word "pattern" when used to mean a combination of stitches, such as **STOCKINETTE STITCH** or **SEED STITCH**, that creates a particular knitted fabric. *See also In Patt.*

Pb

This abbreviation is used to refer to multiple techniques. You will be able to determine which technique to use from context, or by reading your pattern's abbreviations list.

Pb most often signifies purl into the back of the stitch, described under **PTBL**. This produces a twisted stitch, but does not add a new stitch to the row.

Pb is also sometimes used to mean purl in the row below, in the sense of a **LIFTED INCREASE**. An alternate form of purling in the row below is used to create an elongated stitch for decorative effect in certain stitch patterns.

Pb can also mean to purl with a bead. Refer to your pattern's instructions for more information on purling with beads.

Pfb
See P1f&b.

Pick/Picking
See Continental style.

Pick Up/Pick up and knit
See PU/PU and K.

Pick up loops

British term for picking up a dropped stitch.

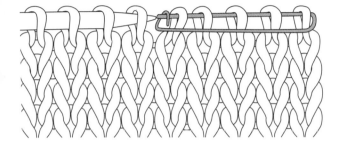

Place stitches on holder

A pattern might tell you to slip stitches off the needle and onto a holder in order to save them as LIVE STITCHES while you do something else. To keep the stitches from unraveling, you can use a piece of WASTE YARN, a spare double-pointed needle with a POINT PROTECTOR at each end, or a device like a large safety pin called a STITCH HOLDER (see above). If you are using a stitch holder, you may find that loops you need to access first are the ones at the far end of the holder. In this case, slide the stitches to a double-pointed needle, and work them from the double-pointed needle. Or you can buy double-ended holders that eliminate this step.

Ply

Most yarns are composed of multiple strands of spun fiber that have been twisted, or plied, together to make a thicker yarn. A 2-ply yarn would have two strands twisted around each other. A 4-ply yarn would have four.

2-PLY YARN

In British, Australian, and New Zealand yarn weight systems, a ply was once a standard width and therefore a 2-ply yarn was understood to be a certain thickness, as was a 4-ply, an 8-ply, and a 12-ply. The term ply is still used sometimes in these countries to describe the weight of a yarn, but it no longer has a direct relationship to the actual number of strands that make up the yarn. See Yarn Weight Equivalents on page 202.

Point protector

*Point protectors are
small rubber caps that
are placed on the
ends of knitting needles
to keep stitches from
falling off and to keep
the points from poking
other things or getting
damaged themselves.
A double-pointed needle
with point protectors
on each end can also be
used as a STITCH HOLDER.
Point protectors are sold
in a variety of sizes to fit
needles of different sizes.*

Plain

Knit plain is an ambiguous term
sometimes found in older patterns
that can mean just work knit stitches,
abandoning any prior patterning,
or it can mean continue working in
the established pattern, without
making any increases or decreases.
If you are not sure of the meaning
of the term in your pattern, study
any accompanying photos to figure
out what is intended.

Plain knitting
An old term for GARTER STITCH.

Ply
See left.

Point protector
See left.

Pm – **Place marker**
See Stitch marker.

Pom-pom

A fluffy ball of yarn used as an embellishment, such as at the top of a hat or the ends of a drawstring.

To begin, make two cardboard doughnuts by cutting two circles as large as you would like your pom-pom, then cutting a hole into the center of each one. Hold the two doughnuts together and, using your fingers or a yarn needle, wrap the yarn around their outer rims until the doughnut hole is full (the more yarn you wrap, the fuller the pom-pom will be). With scissors, cut through the outside edge of the yarn between the disks to make a bundle.

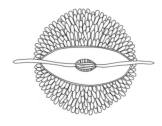

Tightly tie a piece of yarn around the center of the bundle in between the two disks. Remove the cardboard, and fluff up the pom-pom. Trim with scissors, if desired.

Prev – **Previous**

Preparation row

A preparation row is a row that you work once in order to get ready to work subsequent rows. For example, you may work a specific sequence of knits and purls in preparation for a cabled stitch pattern. Or, when knitting circularly, you may work a partial round in order to shift the beginning of rounds from one point on the project to another—for example, from the center of a sock's sole to the division between the sole and instep stitches, in preparation for knitting the toe.

Project yarn

A term sometimes used in contrast to **WASTE YARN**; *see* also *Working yarn*.

Ptbl –
Purl through back loop

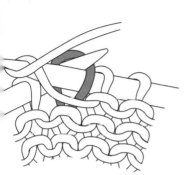

This technique creates a twisted stitch, similar to a KTBL.

To purl a stitch through its back loop, place the right-hand needle behind the work and insert it from behind the back leg of the stitch. Bring the yarn around the right-hand needle as for an ordinary purl stitch. Pull the needle out through the same path and slide the old loop off the left-hand needle.

Provisional cast-on

A provisional cast-on, also known as an invisible or open cast-on, is used when a design calls for going back to add on knitting to a cast-on edge. It is also used if a particular finishing technique requires having LIVE STITCHES, or unworked loops. *See Crochet provisional cast-on and Waste-yarn provisional cast-on.*

Psso – Pass slipped stitch over

This is part of a technique to decrease the number of stitches on the needle. For example, the instructions may direct you to SLIP a stitch knitwise, to knit the next stitch, then to pass the slipped stitch over the knitted one and off the right needle so the slipped stitch encircles the knit stitch. This is the left-leaning decrease known as SKP. Other uses for psso are in the completion of BOBBLES, and in binding off *(see BO).*

Purl
See P.

PW/Pwise – Purlwise
See As if to purl.

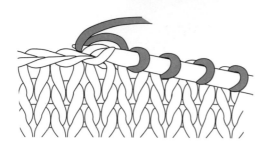

....

PU/PU and K —
Pick up/Pick up and knit

Pick up and knit means to create new stitches along the edge of a fabric by pulling new loops of yarn through the fabric from back to front (as when knitting). Likewise, pick up and purl means to create new stitches by pulling new loops from front to back (as when purling). "Pick up" alone, without an "and knit" or "and purl" qualifier, is unclear: In most cases, it means "pick up and knit," but in some it means to slip part of an edge onto your needles without using the working yarn at all.

To pick up and knit stitches along the edge of a piece of fabric, hold the fabric with the right (or public) side facing you, and begin at the right-hand side of the fabric. Insert the tip of your needle from front to back into the edge of the fabric, under two strands of yarn (inserting under one strand will cause that strand to stretch and distort). Wrap the yarn around the tip of the needle, and pull the yarn forward to the front of the fabric (as you would normally for a knit stitch). Repeat at regular intervals across the width of the fabric.

Another method is to use a crochet hook to pick up the stitches and then to transfer them to a knitting needle.

Your pattern will give you the number of stitches to pick up
and knit. It is helpful to divide the piece into sections and
mark them off with safety pins or pieces of yarn so that you
can add the new stitches evenly across the piece. For example,
if you are to pick up 100 stitches, you would fold the piece
in half, and put a marker at the center, then in the center of
each half, dividing the edge into quarters. You would then
pick up 25 stitches in each quarter.

R

Raglan

Term for a type of sleeve with a prominent slanted seam that extends from the neck to the underarm. Because the sleeve construction has implications for the shape of the body pieces, the entire sweater with this type of sleeve is often called a raglan sweater.

R – **Right**

This may refer to the right-hand needle, usually the empty needle onto which you are knitting new stitches. It may also refer to the right side of a garment as opposed to the left side—that is, to the side on your right when you wear the garment. Finally, it can also refer to the outside or "public side" of a garment; when used in this sense, the term is usually abbreviated **RS**.

Raglan
See above.

Raised increase
See Lifted increase.

RC – **Right cross**
This is a cable crossing that twists up and to the right. *See Cable.*

Reattach yarn
See Attach a new ball of yarn.

Rem – **Remaining**

Rep — Repeat

One meaning for "rep" is the instruction to repeat something, as in "rep from *" or "rep rows 1-4."

Another meaning is a sequence of stitches or rows that forms one complete element of a stitch pattern. In written instructions, repeats are often denoted with asterisks. In charted instructions, they are often denoted with bold lines or brackets. You can place **STITCH MARKERS** on your needles between the repeats to keep track of where they begin and end.

In the following stitch pattern, for example, columns of knit stitches alternate with columns of **GARTER STITCH**. The sequence of five stitches that gets duplicated across each row is the stitch pattern's stitch repeat. Together, the two rows of the pattern form its row repeat.

Instructions Written Out in Words
Row 1 (RS): *K2, p3, repeat from * to last 2 sts, k2.
Row 2 (WS): Purl.

Instructions in Chart Form

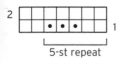

5-st repeat

☐ K on RS, p on WS

• P on RS, k on WS

Rep from *
*See * on page 25.*

Repeat
See Rep.

Reposition stitches onto dpns
See Divide stitches evenly on 3 or 4 needles.

Rev St st – **Reverse Stockinette stitch**
This is the bumpy side of **STOCKINETTE STITCH,** a fabric with smooth V's on one side and bumps on the other. If a pattern calls for Reverse Stockinette stitch, purl on the right (or public) side of the fabric, and knit on the wrong side. If you are working in the round, purl every round.

Reverse single crochet
See Crab stitch.

Reverse shaping
This term is most often used in patterns for wearables, such as vests and sweaters, to tell the knitter to do the opposite of the shaping done in a previous section. Rather than write out the directions for both sides of a garment, patterns often provide complete directions for one side, then simply tell you to reverse shaping for the other side. For example, suppose the left front is worked first, with instructions like "dec 1 st at neck edge every 4 rows 14 times." This means decreasing at the *end* of right-side rows. To reverse shaping for the right front, you'd decrease at the *beginning* of right-side rows.

Some knitters write out row-by-row directions for the second side using the directions for the first side as a guide. Others draw a **SCHEMATIC,** with measurements and the number of stitches in each row so they can check it against the knitting.

Reverse Stockinette stitch
See Rev St st.

RH – **Right hand**

RHN – **Right-hand needle**

1X1 RIB

2X2 RIB

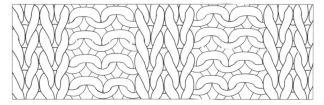

Rib/Ribbing

Ribbing is a type of fabric that lays flat and stretches horizontally. It is often used to keep edges from curling or where a section of a garment needs to pull in and/or be elastic (such as at the cuff of a sleeve).

Ribbing is made by alternating knit and purl stitches to form columns. A simple rib is knit 1, purl 1 ribbing, but varying the number of stitches in the knit and purl columns produces different effects.

If the directions for a rib are abbreviated, you might see something like "2x2 rib" or "4x2 rib." The first number refers to the number of knit stitches, the second to the number of purl stitches. A 4x2 rib would be four knit stitches followed by two purl stitches.

Ridge

A ridge is a horizontal row of bumps created by working two rows of **GARTER STITCH**. One ridge is equal to two rows of Garter stitch.

Right-hand hold

This refers to holding the yarn in the right hand, **AMERICAN STYLE**, as opposed to the left, which is called **CONTINENTAL STYLE**.

Right lifted increase

See RLI.

Right side

See RS.

Right side facing/RS facing

This indicates that the public side of the garment should be facing you.

Right sides together

This indicates that the public sides should be facing each other, so the nonpublic sides are facing outwards. A pattern will sometimes tell you to put the right sides together when you are about to sew two garment pieces together.

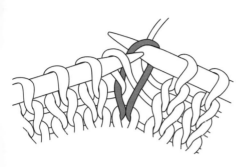

. . . .

RLI –
Right lifted increase

This inconspicuous increase results in a stitch that slants to the right of an existing stitch.

To make a right lifted increase, knit into the top of the stitch below the next stitch on the left needle, leaving the next stitch on the left needle. You have just completed the increase, and are ready to work the next stitch.

The mirror-image counterpart to RLI is LLI.

LOCKING ROW
MARKERS

SPLIT-RING
MARKERS

Row marker

A row marker is a device that you set into a row to help you keep track of your knitting. It is especially handy when you need a point from which to measure length, or when you need to keep track of increases, decreases, cable crossings, or other stitch manipulations. A row marker can be a piece of waste yarn, a safety pin, or a commercially available locking or split-ring marker.

See page 20 for other ideas on how to keep track of your rows.

....

Rnd – **Round**

One round in circular knitting is equal to one row in flat, back-and-forth knitting. When knitting in the round, if you have worked all the stitches in one circuit and are back to where you started, you have worked one round.

Row

In flat knitting (also known as knitting back and forth), working a row means working all the stitches on one needle. To continue, turn the work and begin the next row.

**BARREL-SHAPED
ROW COUNTER**

Row counter

A tool that helps you keep track of the number of rows you have knitted. One type of barrel-shaped row counter sits on the end of a needle when you are working flat (not in the round) and, as you complete each row, you move the counter up one notch. Another type is a separate tool with a button you click; this is sometimes called a kacha-kacha for the sound it makes.

See page 20 for other ideas on how to keep track of your rows.

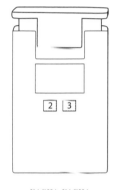

**KACHA-KACHA
ROW COUNTER**

RS – Right side

The right side is the outside or public side of a garment or fabric, in contrast to wrong side, which is the inside, or nonpublic side. We might say a sweater is right-side out as opposed to inside out.

If you are working in GARTER STITCH or another reversible pattern, you can choose which will be the right side. Mark this side with a piece of yarn or a safety pin to make it easier to follow instructions that refer to the right side of the fabric.

S

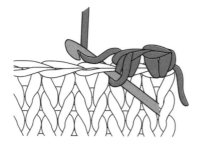

Sc — Single crochet

Single crochet is a simple crochet stitch that can be used to create a firm edge on a knitted piece, such as an afghan or a neck edge.

Attach the yarn to the hook with a **SLIP KNOT**. Starting at the right edge of the piece, *insert the crochet hook into the fabric from front to back, draw up a loop by catching yarn on hook (as shown above) and pulling hook and yarn back through to front of fabric where it entered, yarn over hook and draw the yarn through both loops on the hook, move one stitch to the left and repeat from *.

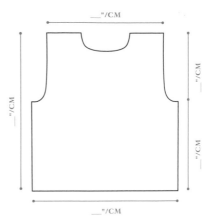

S2kp – **Slip 2, knit 1, pass slipped stitches over**

This is a double decrease that reduces three stitches to one. Because the middle of the three stitches lies on top, the decrease doesn't slant either right or left, and is called a "centered" double decrease.

To work an s2kp, SLIP 2 stitches as if to knit them together—that is, insert the right-hand needle from left to right into both stitches at the same time, and slip them to the right-hand needle. Knit the next stitch. Then, with the tip of the left-hand needle, pass the two slipped stitches over the knit stitch and off the right needle.

This decrease is sometimes abbreviated sl2-k1-p2sso.

Schematic

A schematic is a diagram that gives the dimensions of the finished piece in inches and/or centimeters. Schematics are useful because they can help you determine which size to knit, how the pieces are shaped, and where you might need to alter the pattern. They also show you the dimensions to which each piece should be BLOCKED *before* SEAMING.

Seam/Seaming

Seaming means to sew two pieces together.

Typically, you seam with a YARN NEEDLE *and the same yarn you used to make the pieces. Sometimes, however, seaming is easier if you substitute an alternate yarn. If your project yarn is a fuzzy mohair, or a bumpy bouclé or novelty yarn, substitute a smooth, plain yarn in a matching color to make it easier to draw the yarn through the pieces as you seam. If your project yarn is especially heavy, substitute a ligher-weight yarn to keep the seam from becoming overly bulky.*

Most seams begin with a figure-eight (see top right): Place the right (or public) sides of the two pieces face up, next to each other on a table top or flat surface. Bring a threaded yarn needle up through the lowest loop, from back to front, on the bottom of one piece, leaving a 6-8" (15-20.5 cm) tail. Then bring the needle up through the lowest loop on the other piece. End by bringing the yarn back to the first piece, closing up the figure-eight.

Use the table at right to help you decide which seaming method to use in a particular situation.

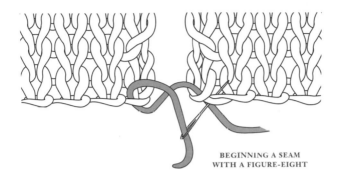

**BEGINNING A SEAM
WITH A FIGURE-EIGHT**

CHOOSING A SEAMING METHOD

IF YOU WANT...	THEN USE ...
to join two selvages (side edges) in a strong, nearly invisible seam with minimal bulk	MATTRESS STITCH
to join two selvages (side edges) in a flat, reversible seam with no bulk	EDGE-TO-EDGE SEAM
to join the end of a piece to an edge—for example, a bound-off shoulder to an armhole edge	VERTICAL-TO-HORIZONTAL SEAM
to join two pieces in a strong, inelastic seam where bulk does not matter (for example, in a bag that will be felted) or where you need to take in extra width	BACKSTITCH
to join two sets of live stitches in a strong, inelastic seam—for example, at the shoulder	THREE-NEEDLE BIND OFF
to join two sets of live stitches invisibly and flexibly	KITCHENER STITCH

NOTE: For instructions on how to work each type of seam, look it up in this book by its specific name.

Seed stitch

Seed stitch is a stitch pattern made by alternating knit and purl stitches. It's reversible, with a bumpy/pebbly surface. It's non-curling, and so can be used as an edging. Many knitters like to use it with variegated yarns, as it breaks up the stripes that would otherwise appear.

To work Seed stitch, alternate knit 1 and purl 1 across the first row, ending with an extra knit 1 if the stitch count is odd. On every subsequent row, knit the purl stitches and purl the knit stitches of the previous row.

Secure ends
See Weave in ends.

Seed stitch
See above.

Selv – **Selvage/Selvedge/ Selvedge edge**
A term for the vertical (rather than cast-on or bound-off) edges of a knitted piece.

One common way to work selvages is to slip the first stitch of every row. This produces an attractive "chain" appearance along the knitted edge. It is suitable for edges that will not be sewn to something else, such as the edges of scarves.

Another common way to work selvages is to knit the first and last stitch on each right-side row (that is, the public side), and to purl them on each wrong-side row. This produces a sturdy **STOCKINETTE** selvage. It is recommended for pieces that will be seamed, such as the front, back, and sleeves of a sweater.

If the pattern calls for increasing or decreasing, do so one or more stitches in from the edges. This leaves the selvage intact, maintaining the appearance of a chain selvage and making a Stockinette selvage easier to seam.

Note: Some knitters find that their selvage stitches are uneven, with the stitches of one row noticeably looser than those of the next row. This is called "rowing out," and it's caused by extra yarn being carried from stitch to stitch as you knit. This extra yarn allows you to have both needles in a stitch temporarily as you work the stitch, but it gets deposited at the end of a row when you turn to work back in the opposite direction. To minimize rowing out and keep your selvages as even as possible, work your stitches close to the tips of your needles, work the first few stitches of each row more tightly than usual, and work the last few a bit more loosely than usual.

Set-in Sleeves

Sweaters with set-in sleeves have armholes and sleeves shaped to fit the wearer's body closely,

creating a smooth, tailored appearance. The curved top portion of the sleeve, known as the sleeve CAP, fits neatly into the armhole like a 3-D jigsaw puzzle. Sewing the cap into the armhole is known as "setting in" the sleeve.

It is helpful to baste the cap into place before sewing it permanently, as this lets you adjust the fit as necessary.

. . . .

Sep – Separately

This term is used in several ways.

If a pattern says to "slip 2 stitches separately" from one needle to the other, you would SLIP 1 stitch to the new needle and then slip the next stitch to the new needle, as opposed to slipping them both at the same time.

If a pattern for a sweater or tank top says to "work each side separately" after binding off stitches for the base of a neck opening, you will need to attach a second ball of yarn so the two pieces (the left front and the right front) are connected only at the base of the neck opening. It is common for patterns to omit the direction to attach a new ball of yarn because it is assumed that the knitter knows that work separately means to work from two separate balls. *See Work(ing) both sides at once.*

Set-up row
See Preparation row.

Sew/Sew together
See Seam/Seaming.

Sew in a sleeve
See Vertical-to-horizontal seaming.

Shape/Shaping
In knitting, shaping refers to using carefully planned increases and decreases to create a particular contour. For example, shaping the crown of a hat knitted from brim up means to make decreases at intervals so that it fits the curve of the head.

Short row(ing)
Short rowing is a technique for adding extra room in one portion of a knitted fabric, in order to create a cuplike shape (for example, for bust darts or sock heels) or to shape the cast-on or bind-off edge of a fabric (for example, to create a shirttail hem or to shape smooth shoulders). Short rowing involves turning your work in the middle of a row while stitches still remain on your left-hand needle—hence the name *short row*—and working back in the opposite direction. To prevent a gap from forming in your work at the point of a short-row turn, you need to *wrap and turn—see W&T.*

Single ply
Yarn made of a single strand of spun fiber. *See Ply.*

Strictly speaking, "single ply" is a misnomer. Plying—that is, twisting multiple strands together—can produce 2-ply or 3-ply yarns, or yarns of even more plies. But in the absence of plying, a yarn composed of a single strand is best known as a "singles" yarn.

Size(s)
Most often the word size in patterns refers to the dimensions of the finished item, as in small, medium, and large. If a size is given in inches and/or centimeters for a garment, it is the measurement across the chest or bust unless otherwise noted.

Size can also apply to needles. Needle size refers to the diameter of the needle.

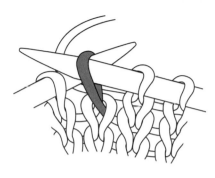

Sl – Slip

To slip means to pass the stitch from one needle to the other without knitting it. You may slip a stitch in preparation for a decrease or to create a particular texture. When slipping stitches, pay careful attention to where the working yarn is located because its location when you slip will affect the look of the finished stitch.

If your pattern says to slip a stitch with no other instruction, hold the yarn to the wrong side of the work, insert your right needle into the stitch as if you were going to purl it, and slip it onto the right needle (as shown above).

If the instructions say slip as if to knit, keep the yarn to the wrong side, insert the needle as if you were going to knit it, then slip it from one needle to the other without actually knitting it.

If the pattern says to slip stitches separately, slip them one at a time.

Sk2p – Slip 1, knit 2 together, pass slipped stitch over

This is a double decrease that reduces three stitches to one and slants to the left. (It is sometimes abbreviated sl1-k2tog-psso.)

To work an sk2p, SLIP a stitch as if to knit. Knit the next 2 stitches together. Then, with the tip of the left-hand needle, pass the slipped stitch over the k2tog and off the right needle.

Skp – Slip 1, knit 1, pass slipped stitch over

This is a decrease that reduces two stitches to one and slants to the left. Like SSK, it is a mirror-image of K2TOG. Choosing between skp and ssk is largely a matter of personal preference.

To work an skp, SLIP a stitch as if to knit. Knit the next stitch. Then, with the tip of the left-hand needle, pass the slipped stitch over the knit stitch and off the right needle.

This decrease is sometimes abbreviated sl1-k1-psso.

Skpo
See Skp.

Sl – Slip
See left.

Sl1-k1-psso
See Skp.

Sl1-k2tog-psso
See Sk2p.

Sl2-k1-p2sso
See S2kp.

Sl M
See Sm.

Sleeve cap
See Cap.

Slightly stretched

This term is sometimes used when measuring a piece of knitted fabric worked in a stitch pattern that is elastic, such as RIBBING. It is usually applied when the fabric is ultimately intended to stretch to fit a particular size. *See Step 8 of Measuring Gauge on page 84.*

Slip
See left.

Slip knot

A slip knot is an adjustable loop. Most CAST-ON methods begin with a slip knot that acts as the first cast-on stitch. If you need to start over, it's easy to pull out a slip knot.

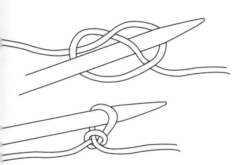

To make a slip knot, lay the yarn on a flat surface and make a pretzel shape. Slip a needle under the strand at the bottom of the pretzel, as shown. Pull on the yarn ends: One will close the knot at the base, and the other will adjust the size of the loop.

....

Slip/Slip stitch
See Sl.

Slip marker
See Sm.

Sm – **Slip marker**
This means you should transfer the **STITCH MARKER** from the left-hand needle to the right-hand needle.

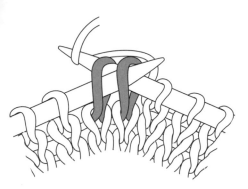

....

Ssk — Slip, slip, knit

This is a decrease that reduces two stitches to one and slants to the left. Like SKP, it is a mirror-image of K2TOG. Choosing between SKP and SSK is largely a matter of personal preference.

To work an ssk, SLIP a stitch AS IF TO KNIT, then slip another stitch as if to knit so both stitches are on the right-hand needle. Guide the left-hand needle from left to right through the front legs of both stitches, and knit them together through their back loops as if they were one stitch.

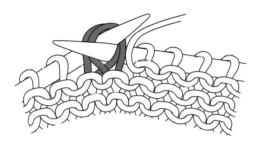

Ssp – Slip, slip, purl

This is a method of reducing the number of stitches on the needles. It produces a purl stitch that slants to the left.

With the yarn in front of your work, **SLIP** a stitch **AS IF TO KNIT**, then slip another stitch as if to knit. Slip these two stitches back to the left-hand needle by inserting the left-hand needle into them from left to right. Then bring the right-hand needle behind the work, and insert it from left to right into the backs of both stitches. Purl them together as if they were one stitch.

Ssp is the converse of **SSK**—that is, working ssp on one side of the fabric is the same as working ssk on the other side. The mirror-image counterpart of ssp is **P2TOG**.

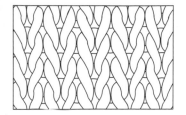

St st — Stockinette stitch

Stockinette stitch is the fabric you create as you alternate one row of knit stitches with one row of purl stitches when knitting flat, or as you knit all stitches in the round. One side is composed of a set of smooth Vs (this is often—but not always—considered the right side); the other side (called REVERSE STOCKINETTE STITCH) is composed of small bumps. It tends to curl forward at its top and bottom edges, and backward at its side edges.

. . . .

St/Sts – Stitch(es)

The word "stitch" has multiple meanings in knitting, depending on context.

In the most narrow sense, a stitch is a loop of yarn on your needles.

"Stitch" can also refer to a stitch maneuver, a way of producing a new loop of yarn on your right-hand needle—for example, a knit stitch, a purl stitch, a yarn over, or a k2tog.

A stitch pattern is a sequence of stitch manuevers that produces a knitted fabric with certain characteristics. For example, combining knit and purl stitches in different ways produces Stockinette stitch, Garter stitch, Seed stitch, or Ribbing. Used in this sense, "stitch" is shorthand for "stitch pattern;" for example, "Stockinette stitch" is short for "Stockinette stitch pattern."

SAFETY PIN–STYLE STITCH HOLDER

DOUBLE-ENDED STITCH HOLDER

Stitch holder

A stitch holder is a device to hold LIVE STITCHES *so they won't unravel. Some stitch holders look like large safety pins and open on one end; others are double-ended. In the absence of a stitch holder, you can improvise by placing live stitches on a piece of* WASTE YARN, *or on a spare double-pointed needle with* POINT PROTECTORS *at each end.*

....

Star – Asterisk, *
*See * on page 25.*

Steek

A steek is a column of stitches inserted into a circularly-knit project so that you may later cut it open to create an opening in your knitting. Steeks are used most often in **STRANDED** knitting, as they allow you to face the right (front) side of stranded color patterning continuously while knitting, and later create

armholes, neck openings, or even the center-front opening of a cardigan.

Before a steek is cut open, its stitches are typically secured to prevent unraveling. A popular method for securing steek stitches involves machine sewing, but approaches using hand-sewing or a crochet hook are also shown in some reference books.

Stitch(es)
See St/Sts.

LOCKING RING
MARKERS

SPLIT-RING
MARKERS

RING
MARKERS

Stitch marker

A stitch marker is a device used to mark a place in your knitting.

If you need to mark a place between stitches, such as the boundary between two pattern **REPEATS**, you can use a small plastic ring (aptly called a ring marker). This ring sits on the needle and is slipped from one needle to the other as you work. If you don't have this type of stitch marker, you can improvise with small rubber bands (the type that are used in orthodontia), pieces of **WASTE YARN** tied in loops, or plastic straws snipped into ringlets.

If you need to mark a stitch itself—for example, when working decreases on each side of a center stitch—you can use a split-ring marker (a ring marker with a tiny opening that allows it to be placed on the yarn or removed from it whenever necessary) or a locking ring marker (also known as a clip-on marker). Or, you can improvise with a safety pin or a piece of waste yarn.

Stockinette stitch
See St st.

Stocking stitch
British term for Stockinette stitch.

Straight needles
Straight needles are knitting needles with points at one end and caps or bulbs at the other. Straight in this case is in contrast to **CIRCULAR** or **DOUBLE-POINTED NEEDLES**.

Stranding
See right.

Superwash
Term applied to wool yarn that has been chemically treated to prevent shrinking and matting (*see Felting/Fulling*). Superwash wool yarns can typically be machine-washed and -dried; see your **YARN LABEL** for care instructions specific to your yarn.

Swatch
A swatch is a test piece of knitted fabric made before you begin a project, usually created so you can test the **GAUGE,** or number of stitches per inch achieved with a certain size needle. To swatch means to create a test piece.

Besides determining gauge, swatching is also good for testing a yarn's washability, color-fastness, and wearability; for practicing a complex stitch pattern before beginning a project, or determining how a stitch pattern looks with a particular yarn; and for determining whether a yarn under consideration for a felting project will actually felt.

Switch to/Change to
Usually refers to changing to a new color—for example, "switch to CC" means to change from working with the **MAIN COLOR** to working with the **CONTRASTING COLOR**. *See Attach a new ball of yarn* if you are just adding this color.

"Switch to" (or "change to") is also used when changing needle size or stitch pattern. *See Change to larger/smaller needles.*

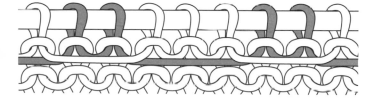

Stranding

Stranding is a colorwork technique in which multiple colors of yarn (usually two, but sometimes more) are used in each row, with the colors not currently in use carried loosely on the wrong side of the fabric. These loose strands, also known as floats, must be secured when they span more than about five stitches. *See Weave Floats.*

T

Tassel

A decorative element
made of strands of yarn
tied at one end.

To make a tassel, wind yarn
around a piece of cardboard
of the desired length. Slide
a piece of yarn under the
wound strands, and use it to
tie the strands together
firmly at the top edge of the
cardboard. Cut the strands
at the bottom edge.

Tie another length of yarn
around the group of strands
about 1 inch below the top
and hide the ends inside the
tassel. Trim the ends, if
desired. Use the free
ends at the top to tie the
tassel to the item for
which it was made.

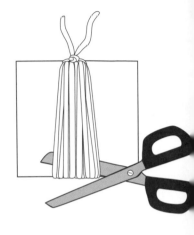

T – Tag end
British term for the **TAIL END** of a yarn, the end not connected to the ball.

Tail/Tail end
The end of a length of yarn that's not attached to a ball—for example, the end remaining after casting on or adding in a new color, or the end left after binding off and cutting the yarn. Used in contrast to ball end or working end.

Yarn ends are usually hidden after a piece is finished (*see Weave in ends*) or used to sew **SEAMS**.

Tapestry needle
See Yarn needle.

Tassel
See left.

Tbl – Through back loop(s)
An instruction to work with the loops on the back of the left-hand needle, rather than the loops in front. *See K2togtbl and P2togtbl.*

Working through the back loop of a conventionally **MOUNTED** stitch causes that stitch to become twisted. This can be done either to tighten the stitch, or for decorative effect. *See Ktbl and Ptbl.*

Some decrease methods involve working stitches through their back loops after slipping the stitches to re-orient them to unconventional mounting. The resulting stitches are not twisted. *See Ssk and Ssp.*

Tension
A British term for **GAUGE**.

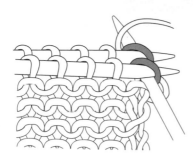

Three-needle bind-off

This is a technique that binds off and joins two pieces of knitting at the same time, and is often used for shoulder seams because it creates a firm, nonstretchy seam.

To begin, line up the two pieces of knitting either with right (public) sides or wrong (nonpublic) sides facing each other (right sides together will create a seam with a "furrow" on the right side; wrong sides together will create a chained ridge on the right side). With the needles next to each other and facing the same way, and with the stitches near the tips, guide a third needle into the first stitch on the needle closest to you, then into the first stitch of the other needle so it picks up the front legs of each stitch. Knit them together as if they were one stitch. Knit another stitch, again through both pieces. You should have two stitches on the third needle. Slip the right-most stitch over the left-most stitch to **BIND OFF**. Continue knitting two stitches together and then binding them off across the row, working loosely so the seam will not pucker.

Twist

When working in INTARSIA, instructions may tell you to twist the yarns at each color change. This means that after you complete a sequence of stitches in one color, you pick up the new yarn for the next color

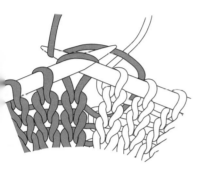

from under the old yarn of the previous color. This joins the two colors, and prevents a hole from forming at the color change.

When STRANDING, you may need to secure long floats (the unworked strands that run across the back of the work). This is sometimes called twisting. *See Weave floats* for details.

....

Tog – **Together**

Transfer stitches

To slide the stitches from a needle or a stitch holder to another needle without working them. Slipping each stitch AS IF TO PURL keeps the stitches MOUNTED conventionally.

Turn

An instruction to flip your work so you are looking at its other side, ready to work back in the opposite direction.

A pattern might tell you to turn your knitting in the middle of a row. It may feel strange the first time you do it, but the directions are, in fact, telling you to turn the work without finishing the entire row. This appears in directions for SHORT ROW(ING).

Twist
See above.

Two-tail cast-on
See Long-tail cast-on.

U

Unravel

As in English, to unravel in Knitspeak means to pull apart. For example, instructions may tell you to unravel a CROCHET PROVISIONAL CAST-ON. Unraveling can also refer to the process of ripping out a section of knitting, to recover from a mistake. *For more on ripping out, see page 210.*

Using smaller/larger needles

An instruction to change to another needle size.

Many garment patterns make use of needles of two sizes: smaller needles for cuffs, neckbands, and other ribbing, for firmness; and larger needles for the majority of the fabric, for a more fluid feel. You may see the instruction to use needles of the smaller or larger size when casting on, or when picking up stitches for trim such as buttonbands.

Usually, GAUGE (the number of stitches and rows per inch) is specified for the larger needles. If you need to adjust the size of these larger needles to match gauge, also adjust the size of the smaller needles accordingly. *See Change to larger/smaller needles.*

Using MC/CC

An instruction to use yarn of either the main color (MC) or a contrasting color (CC). You may see this instruction when casting on, or when picking up stitches for trim such as buttonbands. *See Switch to/Change to.*

V

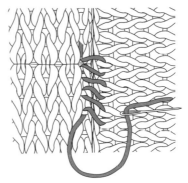

Vertical-to-horizontal seaming

This finishing technique for attaching stitches to rows is most often used when attaching the bound-off edge of one piece to the selvage (or side edge) of another piece, such as when sewing a bound-off sleeve to the selvage of an armhole.

Place both pieces on a flat surface with right (public) sides facing you. Arrange so sleeve is perpendicular to the body, and sits in the armhole. Pin the center of the **SLEEVE CAP** to the shoulder seam, then pin the rest of sleeve into armhole so it fits comfortably in armhole curve.

Beginning at the shoulder seam, insert a threaded **YARN NEEDLE** under both halves of a stitch on the sleeve piece, with the tip of the needle pointing towards you as you insert it under the stitch (i.e. pointing downwards). Then, carrying the yarn across to the front of the body, gently tug at the selvage to find the vertical bars between the edge stitches. Guide the needle under one of the horizontal bars, with the needle pointing downwards. Move the yarn needle back to the sleeve, reinserting the needle under both parts of the next stitch. Repeat on each side of seam, until entire seam is worked, being careful not to pull too tightly.

Stitches are typically wider than rows are tall, so for every few stitches of the sleeve you will need to seam an extra row of the armhole. To do this, bring the yarn needle under two bars on the body piece rather than one often enough to keep the seam from puckering. For example, if the pieces were knit in **STOCKINETTE STITCH**, seam 4 rows for every 3 stitches.

WRAP A STITCH

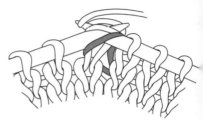

KNIT A WRAP WITH
ITS STITCH

W&T –
Wrap and turn

Wrap and turn is a technique used with SHORT ROWS, a shaping method that involves turning your work in the middle of a row. If you simply turn and work back in the opposite direction without wrapping, you will create a small hole in the fabric. The wrap-and-turn technique prevents these holes from forming.

To wrap a stitch, bring the yarn to the front, SLIP the next stitch as if to purl, bring the yarn to the back, and slip the stitch back to the left needle before turning the work. The wrapped stitch will have a horizontal loop around its base made by the working yarn.

Your pattern will tell you how many short rows to work, and where to wrap and turn. Eventually, you will need to work a stitch that has been wrapped on a previous row. When this happens, *work the wrap with the stitch it wraps.* This keeps

**PURL A WRAP
WITH ITS STITCH**

the wrap from being visible
on the right (public) side of your
work. To knit a wrap with its
stitch, insert the tip of the right-
hand needle under the wrap
at the front of the work, then
into the wrapped stitch, then knit
the two loops together. To purl
a wrap with its stitch, insert
the tip of the right-hand needle
under the wrap at the back
of the work and lift it onto the
left-hand needle, then purl
the wrap and its wrapped
stitch together.

Waste yarn

A length of scrap yarn that
will be pulled out and discard-
ed later, or onto which you
will transfer stitches. When
selecting a waste yarn, choose
a smooth yarn that will not
leave fuzz or tangle easily in
your knitting, such as crochet
cotton, mercerized cotton,
or unwaxed and unflavored
dental floss. Use a contrasting
color that stands out from the
rest of your knitting.

STEP 1

Waste-yarn provisional cast-on

This method of working a PROVISIONAL CAST-ON requires a length of WASTE YARN in addition to your working yarn.

To begin, make a SLIP KNOT at the end of your waste yarn and another at the end of your working yarn, and place them both on a needle. (Note that neither slip knot counts as a stitch; they just serve to hold the yarn ends to the needle temporarily.) Hold the needle in your right hand with the tip pointing up; hold the slip knots in place with your right thumb and forefinger. With your left hand, hold the yarns taut in "slingshot position," with the waste yarn over your left thumb and the working yarn over your left index finger.

step 1

Bring the tip of the needle down in front of the two yarns, under the waste yarn, up between the yarns, over and behind the working yarn, and forward under both yarns.

You have formed a stitch with the working yarn that's secured by the waste yarn.

step 2

Bring the needle over and behind the working yarn again, and up between the two yarns.

You have formed another stitch with the working yarn.

Repeat steps 1 and 2 until there are enough stitches on the needle, not counting the initial slip knots. Work

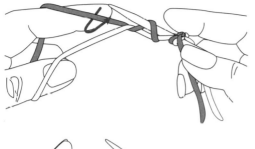

STEP 2

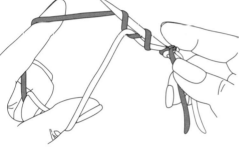

STEPS 1 AND 2
COMPLETED
(2 STITCHES CAST ON)

your first row according to your pattern, then drop the slip knots off the needle at the end of the row.

Later, when you are ready to use live stitches at the cast-on edge, transfer the stitches from the waste yarn to a double-pointed or circular needle one or two sizes smaller than your working needles. As you resume knitting with your working needles, be aware that half the stitches will be **MOUNTED** unconventionally, with their leading loops in back of the needle; to avoid twisting these stitches, turn them around so they are mounted conventionally or simply work them through their **BACK** loops.

See Crochet provisional cast-on for a provisional cast-on made using a crochet chain.

WB

See Wyib.

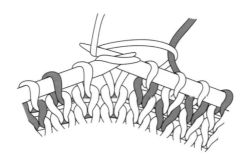

Weave floats

When STRANDING, instructions may tell you to weave in long floats. That is, when working five or more stitches of one color, you need to secure the strand of the other color to the wrong side of the fabric. This minimizes the chance that a loose float will get snagged as you handle or wear your garment.

To secure a float, twist the active and inactive yarn once every few stitches while working with the active yarn.

Weave in ends

This means to hide and secure the tail ends of yarn on the wrong (nonpublic) side of the knitting, along the selvages (edges), or by tracing over stitches with them.

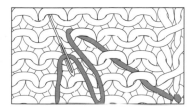

To weave a tail on the wrong side of the knitting, thread the tail onto a YARN NEEDLE and bring it under the bumps formed by several stitches without letting the tail peek through to the right side. Stretch out the knitting as you weave so it does not cause fabric to pucker. If the yarn is thin or slippery, double back to secure the end. Trim the tail close to the knitting. Do not tie a knot; it will leave a bump that can work its way to the right side.

STRATEGIES FOR WEAVING IN ENDS	
IF YOU ...	THEN ...
want to hide the tail on the inside of a garment	on the wrong side, weave the tail under the bumps formed by several stitches, as described above
don't want the yarn tail to show on a reversible item	work the yarn end through the loops along the edges, or use DUPLICATE STITCH to trace over some stitches
have two yarn tails in the same place	weave them in different directions, up and down or right and left
want to hide the tail in the bound-off edge	trace path of loops along the edge

Weave seams

This may be a reference to the general concept of sewing or seaming, or to the specific techniques of KITCHENER STITCH (for joining live stitches) or MATTRESS STITCH (for joining SELVAGES). *See Seam/Seaming* to determine which technique would be the most appropriate to use.

Weaving

Weaving has multiple meanings. It can refer to the process of hiding yarn ends (*see Weave in ends*), to the process of securing long floats or lengths of yarn when stranding (*see Weave floats*), or to seaming (*see Weave seams*).

Weight

See Yarn weight.

Welt

The horizontal version of a rib stitch, formed by alternating a few rows of STOCKINETTE STITCH with a few rows of REVERSE STOCKINETTE STITCH.

WF

See Wyif.

With right/wrong side facing

With right side facing means to hold the piece of knitting so that the side that would face the public is facing you. With wrong side facing means that the inside of the item, or nonpublic side, is facing you.

With right/wrong sides together

With right sides together means holding two pieces of knitting so the public sides are facing each other. With wrong sides together means holding the pieces so the nonpublic sides are facing each other.

WON – **Wool over needle**
British term for YO.

Wool around needle
British term for YO.

Work
To work means to continue in the stitch pattern that has been established. It is often used instead of "to knit" (in the generic sense of creating fabric with knitting needles) to avoid confusion with "to knit" (in the specific sense of knitting rather than purling).

Work across
See Acr – Across.

Work as established
This means to continue to knit (or purl) in the pattern given.

Work as for...
See Work in same manner as...

Work as they appear
To work stitches as they appear means to knit the knit stitches and purl the purl stitches.
See As they appear.

Work(ing) back and forth
This means to knit flat in rows, in contrast to knitting in the round on circular or double-pointed needles.

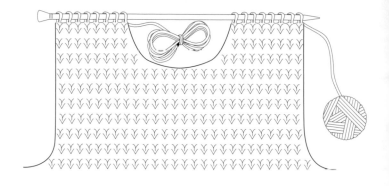

Work(ing) both sides at once

Usually found in patterns for sweaters and tank tops, to work both sides at once means to work the left and right sides of the neck as unconnected pieces. To do this, you will need to work from two separate lengths of yarn. It is common for patterns to omit the direction to ATTACH A NEW BALL OF YARN, but you must do this to keep the pieces separate.

Work each side separately

See Work(ing) both sides at once.

Work even/Work plain/
Work straight

This means to continue creating the pattern stitch that has been established, without increasing or decreasing, until indicated otherwise in the directions.

Work(ing) flat

See Work(ing) back and forth.

Work in same manner as ...

This means to follow the directions for the other referenced piece. For example, instructions for sweaters and vests often start with the back. For the front, they may say something like "Work in same manner as back until piece measures 14 (15, 16)" (35.5 [38, 40.5] cm)," and then give different directions for the rest of the front piece.

Work over __ stitches

This direction tells you to work in the specified pattern for a certain number of stitches.

This may be stated so that you can confirm that you have the correct number. For example if you are making a sweater with 60 stitches, the pattern might say "work in 2x2 rib over 60 stitches." This means you would knit 2 and then purl 2, repeating this sequence for all the stitches on the row, which should be a total of 60.

Or this may be telling you to create a particular stitch pattern over a subset of the stitches. In this case, a pattern for a sweater with 60 stitches might say "work cable pattern over 32 stitches," meaning that the cable panel takes up slightly more than half of the total number of stitches, while another stitch pattern is being worked on the remaining 28 stitches.

Work separately

See Work(ing) both sides at once.

Work to last __ stitches

This means to work in the stitch pattern that has been established until there are only the prescribed number of stitches remaining on the left-hand needle.

Working yarn

This is the strand of yarn that comes from the ball of yarn, as opposed to the tail end of the yarn. If you are knitting with multiple colors, it means the active yarn. The inactive yarn is the color not in use.

The term working yarn is also used sometimes in contrast to **WASTE YARN**—for example, "drop working yarn, k15 with WY, slip these 15 sts back to LHN and continuing with working yarn ..." In this sense, working yarn means the same thing as project yarn.

Wrap and turn

See W&T.

Wrap twice

Some textured stitch patterns may instruct you to wrap twice—for example, "knit next stitch, wrapping yarn around needle twice." This means you wrap the yarn around the right needle twice before pulling these loops forward through the old stitch. Your pattern instructions should tell you what to do with the extra wrap on the subsequent row—for example, it may say to drop the extra wrap, creating an elongated stitch.

WRN – Wool around needle

British term for **YO.**

Wrong side

See WS.

Wrp&T
See W&T.

WS – **Wrong side**
The wrong side is the nonpublic side, the opposite of the right or public side of the knitted piece. For a garment, the wrong side is the inside of the garment. In a pattern, *wrong side out* means inside out. *Wrong sides together* means to place two pieces of knitting so the the nonpublic sides are facing each other (and public sides are facing out).

WY
See Waste yarn.

Wyib – **With yarn in back**
To hold the yarn in the back of the work while you perform the next action.

Wyif – **With yarn in front**
To hold the yarn to the front of the work while you perform the next action.

Y

Yarn

Yarn is the basic raw material used in knitting. It's composed of fibers that have been spun into strands, and then optionally plied together. The characteristics of a particular yarn depend on many factors, including the fibers from which it was spun (wool, cotton, nylon, etc.), how the fibers were prepared prior to spinning (carded or combed), how the strands were spun (tightly or loosely, thick or thin), and how many strands were plied together.

Yarn needle

Also called a tapestry needle, a yarn needle is a needle with a large eye and a blunt (sometimes curved) tip, used for sewing seams and weaving in ends.

To thread yarn through the eye of a yarn needle, fold the yarn over the needle and pinch the fold between thumb and forefinger. Pulling up on the needle to create a sharp fold, slide the needle out of your pinch, leaving the sharply-folded yarn between your fingers. Lower the eye of the needle over the sharp fold.

Yarn over
See YO.

Yarn weight

In a pattern, yarn weight refers to the thickness (or grist) of a yarn. This is often indicated with terms like worsted-weight or DK-weight, or with standard yarn weight symbols.

On a yarn label, yarn weight refers to the quantity of yarn in one ball or skein, as measured in grams or ounces. Most labels also state the length of the yarn in a ball or skein, as measured in yards or meters.

When choosing yarn for a project, select the same yarn called for in the pattern, or substitute a similar yarn. *See page 192 for more information on substituting yarns.*

When determining how much yarn to buy for a project, base your decisions on the number of yards or meters of yarn called for in the pattern. This is more accurate than basing decisions on weight in grams or ounces: Two sweaters of the same size knit from yarns of the same thickness will require the same length of yarn, but if one is wool and the other is cotton, the wool sweater will weigh less than the cotton sweater.

Yb – **Yarn back/Bring yarn to back of work**

This means to bring the yarn between the tips of the two needles to the back of the work.

Yd – **Yard**

Yf – **Yarn forward/Bring yarn to front of work**

This means to bring the yarn between the tips of the two needles to the front of the work.

Yo –
Yarn over

Also called yarn around needle, wool over needle, and wool around needle, this is an INCREASE that creates a decorative hole in the work.

To make a yarn over, bring the working yarn forward between the needle tips, then over the right-hand needle to the back. If you need to purl the next stitch, complete the yarn over, then bring the working yarn forward again between the needle tips, not over the right-hand needle.

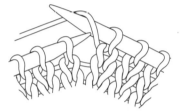

YARN OVER WITH WORKING YARN IN POSITION FOR A KNIT STITCH

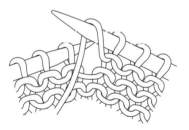

YARN OVER WITH WORKING YARN IN POSITION FOR A PURL STITCH

When you reach this yarn over on the next row, you will encounter a long leg of yarn, slanting to the right. Put your right-hand needle under this long, slanty leg, and work the stitch, opening up a large hole, useful for buttons or for making eyelets when knitting lace.

WORKING YARN OVER ON NEXT ROW

If a pattern calls for a yarn over at the beginning of a row before a knit stitch, bring the yarn to the front of the work before you insert the needle into the first stitch. Then bring the yarn over the right-hand needle before knitting the stitch.

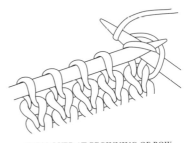

YARN OVER AT BEGINNING OF ROW BEFORE KNIT STITCH

If the pattern calls for a yarn over at the beginning of a row before a purl stitch, bring the yarn to the front of the work, over and behind the right-hand needle, then under the needle to the front again. Purl the next stitch as usual.

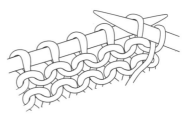

YARN OVER AT BEGINNING OF ROW BEFORE PURL STITCH

Yon – **Yarn over needle**
See YO.

Yrn – **Yarn around needle**
See YO.

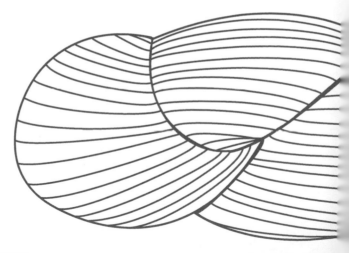

Appendix

190 KNITSPEAK ANATOMY

192 GUIDELINES FOR SUBSTITUTING YARNS

196 HOW TO READ A YARN LABEL

202 YARN WEIGHT EQUIVALENTS

204 ESTIMATING YARN NEEDS

MISTAKES HAPPEN
   208 PICKING UP DROPPED STITCHES
   210 NOTES ON RIPPING OUT

213 WORKSHEETS
   214 PROJECT
   216 PLANNING
   218 SCHEMATIC

219 US/METRIC NEEDLE SIZES

219 METRIC/IMPERIAL CONVERSION EQUATIONS

220 ABBREVIATIONS AT A GLANCE

222 BIBLIOGRAPHY

224 ACKNOWLEDGEMENTS

Knitspeak Anatomy

Here are the terms that knitting patterns use most often for the different parts of sweaters, socks, and mittens.

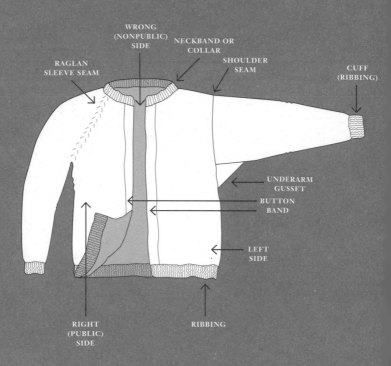

WRONG
(NONPUBLIC)
SIDE

NECKBAND OR
COLLAR

SHOULDER
SEAM

RAGLAN
SLEEVE SEAM

CUFF
(RIBBING)

UNDERARM
GUSSET

BUTTON
BAND

LEFT
SIDE

RIGHT
(PUBLIC)
SIDE

RIBBING

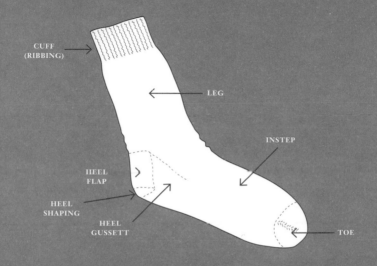

CUFF
(RIBBING)

LEG

INSTEP

HEEL
FLAP

HEEL
SHAPING

HEEL
GUSSETT

TOE

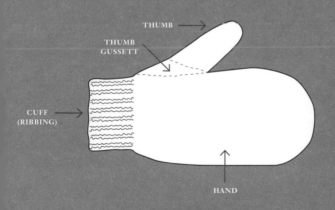

THUMB

THUMB
GUSSETT

CUFF
(RIBBING)

HAND

GUIDELINES FOR SUBSTITUTING YARNS

Most patterns call for a specific yarn. But you can substitute the yarn of your choice, provided that the substitute yarn matches the original in weight and construction. Once you have chosen your substitute, it's easy to figure out how many balls you need to purchase.

Yarn weight

A substitute yarn must match the original yarn in weight—that is, in thickness. Substituting a yarn that's too light in weight (too thin) will result in overly drapey and airy fabric; substituting a yarn that's too heavy in weight (too thick) will result in overly stiff fabric.

To determine if two yarns are of the same weight, compare the recommended GAUGE listed on the yarns' ball bands. Note that a yarn's recommended gauge is the gauge at which the yarn will produce a STOCKINETTE fabric of medium DRAPE—not overly firm, and not overly loose. Keep in mind that your pattern may not be aiming for average or medium drape. For example, if you're making heavy boot socks, your pattern may call for worsted-weight yarn worked at a tight gauge to create a firm fabric. Or, if you're making a drapey shawl, your pattern may call for a worsted-weight yarn worked at a loose gauge to create a light, airy fabric. Thus, it is better to compare the gauge from yarn label to yarn label rather than from pattern to yarn label.

Yarn construction

For best results, a substitute yarn should have a construction similar to that of the original yarn—specifically, it's helpful if the two yarns are similar in elasticity (stretchiness) and texture. For example, you wouldn't want to use a nonstretch (inelastic) cotton yarn to knit a hat pattern designed for a stretchy wool yarn, as the resulting hat might not hug the wearer's head as intended. And you probably wouldn't want to use a fluffy novelty yarn to knit a cabled pattern designed for a smooth yarn, as the fluff would obscure the cable patterning.

To determine if two yarns are of similar construction, compare their fiber content and examine sample garments and **SWATCHES** on display in a yarn shop. If no samples are on display, consider purchasing a single ball of each yarn you are considering and knitting a few swatches of your own.

Number of balls required

To know how much of your substitute yarn to buy, you will need to find out how many yards/meters of the original yarn was suggested. Usually this information is given in the pattern next to the name of the yarn, expressed either in yards/meters or as a number of balls. If it's given as a number of balls, multiply the number of balls by the number of yards/meters in each ball of the original yarn to get the total number of yards/meters required.

| NUMBER OF BALLS OF ORIGINAL YARN CALLED FOR IN PATTERN | X | NUMBER OF YARDS/ METERS IN EACH BALL OF ORIGINAL YARN | = | TOTAL NUMBER OF YARDS/METERS REQUIRED |

Divide the total yards/meters by the number of yards/ meters in each ball of your substitute yarn.

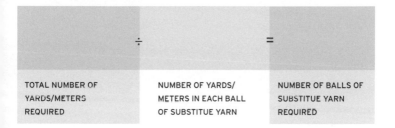

| TOTAL NUMBER OF YARDS/METERS REQUIRED | ÷ | NUMBER OF YARDS/ METERS IN EACH BALL OF SUBSTITUE YARN | = | NUMBER OF BALLS OF SUBSTITUE YARN REQUIRED |

If a pattern does not tell you how many yards or meters are in one ball, ask the shopkeeper, who may be able to look it up in a reference book or call the manufacturer. Or, you might find this information on the Internet. Whether you are substituting yarns or not, it's always a good idea to buy an extra ball. Some stores will allow you to return the extra ball if you don't use it within a certain time period as long as you still have the receipt.

HOW TO READ A YARN LABEL

Most yarn labels contain a wealth of information—if you know how to decipher it.

Fiber content

All yarn labels are supposed to include a list of the fiber content, such as 100% wool, or 50% wool and 50% silk. If you understand the properties of different fibers, this information can help you when determining whether a particular yarn will work in a project. Fiber content may be listed in a foreign language, depending on where the yarn was manufactured. Here are some terms to help you translate:

ENGLISH	FRENCH	GERMAN	ITALIAN	SPANISH
WOOL	LAINE	WOLLE	LANA	LANA
MOHAIR	MOHAIR	MOHAIR	MOHAIR	MOHAIR
CASHMERE	CACHEMIRE	KASCHMIR	CASHMERE	CACHEMIRA
ANGORA	ANGORA	ANGORA	ANGORA	ANGORA
ALPACA	LAINE D'ALPAGA	ALPAKA-WOLLE	LANA D'ALPACA	LANA DE ALPACA
COTTON	COTON	BAUMWOLLE	COTONE	ALGODÓN
LINEN	LIN	LEINEN	LINO	LINO
SILK	SOIE	SEIDE	SETA	SEDA
ACRYLIC	ACRYLIQUE	ACRYL	ACRILICO	ACRÍLICO

GAUGE

10 X 10 CM
4 X 4 INCHES
24 R
18 S

RECOMMENDED NEEDLE SIZE

6 UK
8 US
5mm

MEDIUM
4
WORSTED

WEIGHT CATEGORY SYMBOL

Knitspeak Yarns

ANDREA

MANUFACTURER'S NAME

YARN NAME

ivory | #7

DYE LOT: 0542M

50% COTTON/50% SILK
3.5 OZ (100G)
APPROX. 200 YARDS (192 M)

COLOR NAME/ NUMBER

DYE LOT NUMBER

FIBER CONTENT

QUANTITY, IN LENGTH AND/ OR WEIGHT

30C
P

CARE SYMBOLS

MADE IN U.S.A.

COUNTRY OF ORIGIN

Color and dye lot

A yarn label typically lists both a yarn's color and its DYE LOT number. Sometimes, color is given by a name, such as "Seafoam." Often, however, it is given by a number, such as "3768." When this happens—when the yarn label simply provides two numbers, such as "3768 349"—generally, the first number is the color, and the second is the dye lot.

Recommended needle size and gauge

Most yarn labels provide a recommended needle size and gauge. That is, knitting the yarn in STOCKINETTE STITCH at an average tension on needles of the recommended size ought to produce a fabric with the recommended gauge. This fabric will be of medium DRAPE, suitable for use in a garment.

The recommended needle size is a good starting point at which to begin swatching for gauge, but it is not necessarily the size you should use for knitting your project. You may need to use smaller or larger needles to match the gauge required by your pattern.

The recommended gauge is useful for comparing two yarns—if they have the same recommended gauge and similar fiber content, they can probably be substituted for each other—but it is not necessarily the gauge at which you should knit your project. To ensure that your effort results in an item of the intended size, you must match the gauge required by your pattern.

See Measuring Gauge and Choosing Needle Sizes on page 82 for more information.

Foreign gauge terms

Yarn manufacturers in different parts of the world use different abbreviations in the gauge information found on their yarn labels. Here are some terms to help you translate:

LANGUAGE	STITCH	ROW
ENGLISH	S for stitch	R for row
FRENCH	M for maille	R for rang
GERMAN	M for Masche	R for Reihe
ITALIAN	M for maglia	F for ferrata
SPANISH	P for punto	V for vuelta

Yarn weight and/or length

This information, given in ounces/grams and yards/meters, will help you to figure out how many balls of a particular yarn you need to buy for a project.

Care instructions

Many yarn labels include the international symbols that tell you how to care for your knitted item. A complete set of symbols explains five aspects: washing, bleaching, drying, ironing, and professional cleaning. The temperature for washing is given in degrees Celsius (see Note).

 Wash gently by hand in water not exceeding 30° C.

 Cool iron.

 Do not bleach.

 Do not iron or press.

 Tumble dry.

 Dry-clean, normal cycle. Any solvent except trichloroethylene.

 Do not tumble dry.

 Do not dry-clean.

 Remove excess water and dry flat.

NOTE: To convert Celcius to Fahrenheit, multiply the Celcius temperature by 1.8, then add 32.

Yarn Weight Equivalents

Yarn is put into categories by weight. If you cannot find the pattern's recommended yarn, you will need to substitute another one from the same weight category. For more information on substituting yarns, see page 192.

YARN WEIGHT SYMBOL & CATEGORY NAMES	1 SUPER FINE	2 FINE	3 LIGHT
TYPE OF YARNS IN CATEGORY	SOCK, FINGERING, BABY	SPORT, BABY	DK, LIGHT WORSTED
AUSTRALIAN, BRITISH, NEW ZEALAND EQUIVALENTS IN PLY	3-4 PLY	5-8 PLY	8-PLY
KNIT GAUGE RANGE* IN STOCKINETTE STITCH TO 4" (10 CM)	27-32 STS	23-26 STS	21-24 STS
RECOMMENDED NEEDLE IN METRIC SIZE RANGE	2.25–3.25 MM	3.25–3.75 MM	3.75–4.5 MM
RECOMMENDED NEEDLE US SIZE RANGE AND LARGER	1 TO 3	3 TO 5	5 TO 7

* GUIDELINES ONLY:
This table reflects the most
commonly used gauges and needle
sizes for specific yarn categories.

Adapted from the Yarn
Standards of the Craft Yarn
Council of America

(4) MEDIUM	(5) BULKY	(5) SUPER BULKY
WORSTED, AFGHAN, ARAN	CHUNKY, CRAFT, RUG	BULKY, ROVING
10-12 PLY	12-16 PLY	
16-20 STS	12-15 STS	6-11 STS
4.5–5.5 MM	5.5–8 MM	8 MM AND LARGER
7 TO 9	9 TO 11	11

Estimating Yarn Needs

Use these charts to estimate how much yarn you need for a project if you're obtaining yarn before settling on a specific pattern. Remember that these estimates cannot take into account every variation in size, style, stitch pattern, and knitting preference. (If you are working from a specific pattern, obtain the yarn amount suggested in the pattern.)

SIZE	DK 5½ STS = 1"	WORSTED 4½ STS = 1"	BULKY 3½ STS = 1"
28"–31½" (71–80 cm)	935–1165 yds (855–1065 m)	650–815 yds (595–745 m)	500–625 yds (460–570 m)
32"–34" (81.5–86.5 cm)	1130–1415 yds (1035–1295 m)	820–1025 yds (750–940 m)	625–780 yds (570–715 m)
36"–38" (91.5–96.5 cm)	1250–1565 yds (1145–1430 m)	990–1230 yds (905–1125 m)	750–925 yds (685–845 m)
40"–42" (101.5–106.5 cm)	1425– 1780 yds (1305–1630 m)	1100–1375 yds (1005–1260 m)	875–1095 yds (800–1000m)
44"–46" (112–117 cm)	1600–2000 yds (1465–1830 m)	1210–1515 yds (1105–1385 m)	1000–1250 yds (915–1145 m)
48"–50" (122–127 cm)	1790–2235 yds (1635–2045 m)	1320–1650 yds (1200–1510 m)	1125–1400 yds (1025–1280 m)

Charts on pages 204-207 adapted from *Knit: A Personal Handbook* (STC, 2003)

SIZE	DK 5½ STS = 1"	WORSTED 4½ STS = 1"	BULKY 3½ STS = 1"
NEWBORN– 12 MONTHS 16"–18" (40.5–45.5 cm)	300–400 yds (275–365 m)	250–330 yds (230–300 m)	135–165 yds (125–150m)
12–24 MONTHS 19"–20" (48.5–51 cm)	405–540 yds (370–495 m)	340–425 yds (310–390 m)	180–225 yds (165–205 m)
SIZES 2–5 21"–24" (53.5–61 cm)	495–660 yds (450–600 m)	410–550 yds (375–500 m)	215–265 yds (195–245 m)
SIZES 6–8 25"–27" (63.5–68.5 cm)	775–965 yds (710–885 m)	645–805 yds (590–735 m)	365–455 yds (335–415 m)
SIZES 10–12 28"–30" (71–76 cm)	860–1070 yds (785–980 m)	720–900 yds (660–825 m)	460–575 yds (420–525 m)
SIZES 14–16 31"–32½" (78.5–82.5 cm)	1095–1370 yds (1000–1250 m)	800–1000 yds (730–915 m)	610–760 yds (560–695 m)

HATS
STOCKINETTE STITCH, HEAD CIRCUMFERENCE GIVEN

SIZE	DK 5½ STS = 1"	WORSTED 4½ STS = 1"	BULKY 3½ STS = 1"
BABIES 12"–14" (30.5–35.5 cm)	90–105 yds (80–95 m)	70–80 yds (65–75 m)	55–65 yds (50–60 m)
CHILDREN 16"–19½" (40–49.5 cm)	135–155 yds (125–140 m)	115–125 yds (105–115 m)	70–85 yds (65–80 m)
WOMEN 20" (51 cm)	160–185 yds (145–170 m)	135–155 yds (125–140 m)	105–120 yds (95–110 m)
MEN 22" (56 cm)	190–225 yds (175–205 m)	150–165 yds (140–150 m)	115–130 yds (105–120 m)

SCARVES
GARTER STITCH, NOT INCLUDING FRINGE OR TRIM

SIZE	DK 5½ STS = 1"	WORSTED 4½ STS = 1"	BULKY 3½ STS = 1"
6" x 48" (15 x 122 cm)	375–450 yds (340–410 m)	240–285 yds (220–260 m)	110–135 yds (100–125 m)
8" x 60" (20.5 x 152.5 cm)	635–760 yds (580–695 m)	400–475 yds (365–435 m)	175–225 yds (160–205 m)
10" x 72" (25.5 x 183 cm)	950–1170 yds (870–1070 m)	600–720 yds (550–660 m)	265–335 yds (240–305 m)

SIZE	SOCK 7 STS = 1"	DK 5½ STS = 1"	WORSTED 4½ STS = 1"	BULKY 3½ STS = 1"
BABIES & CHILDREN UP TO US 13 7½" (19 cm)	180–270 yds (165–245 m)	120–200 yds (110–180 m)	100–165 yds (90–150 m)	75–125 yds (70–115 m)
WOMEN US 6½" TO 10" 9"–10¼" (23–26 cm)	310–370 yds (285–340 m)	290–335 yds (265–310 m)	265–300 yds (240–275 m)	160–190 yds (145–175 m)
MEN US 7½" TO 11" 9¾"–11" (25–28 cm)	385–480 yds (350–440 m)	345–410 yds (315–375 m)	310–340 yds (285–310 m)	195–250 yds (180–230 m)

SIZE	DK 5½ STS = 1"	WORSTED 4½ STS = 1"	BULKY 3½ STS = 1"
BABY BLANKET 30" X 30" (76 x 76 cm)	765–880 yds (700–805 m)	625–720 yds (570–660 m)	475–545 yds (435–500 m)
AFGHAN OR SOFA-SIZE 48" x 60" (122 x 152.5 cm)	2450–2815 yds (2240–2575 m)	1945–2235 yds (1780–2045 m)	1365–1570 yds (1250–1435 m)

Mistakes Happen: Dropped Stitches

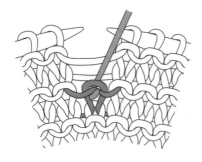

It is inevitable that you will some-times drop stitches unintentionally and they will need to be picked up.

Knit to the point in the row where the dropped stitch appears. If you're re-establishing a stitch on a row that forms a ridge (as shown above), with the horizontal bar in front of the stitch, insert a crochet hook into the loose stitch from the back, hook the loose bar, and pull it through the stitch from front to back.

If your stitch has dropped down several rows, turn the work around and repeat the same process on the other side, working each horizontal bar in the correct order from the bottom up. Continue, turning the work after each row, until you have worked all the way up the ladder of horizontal bars. To finish, place the final stitch on the left-hand needle so the right-hand side of the stitch is in front (*see Mounted*).

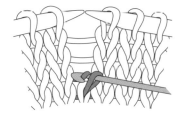

PICKING UP A DROPPED STITCH IN STOCKINETTE STITCH

On the knit (smooth) side of the work, work to the point in the row where the dropped stitch is located. Insert a crochet hook into the dropped stitch from front to back, with the horizontal bar behind the stitch. Hook the horizontal bar, and pull it through the dropped stitch from back to front (as shown above). If your stitch has droppped down several rows, start at the lowest point and repeat until you have picked up all of the loose horizontal bars in the correct order. To finish, place the final stitch on the left-handle needle it the right-hand side of the stitch is in front (*see Mounted*).

If you are working on the purl (bumpy) side and want to pick up dropped stitches, work to the point in the row where the dropped stitch occurs, turn the work around so the knit (smooth) side is facing you, and pick up the dropped stitch from the front side of the work as shown here, then return to the purl side and continue.

Mistakes Happen: Notes on Ripping Out

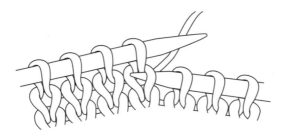

RIPPING OUT ONE STITCH AT A TIME

It can be disturbing to find an error in your work. Depending on its seriousness (one stray purl in the midst of a sea of knit stitches on a rarely seen part of a garment vs. an entire section knit in the wrong stitch pattern), you may or may not want to rip (see page 212). If you decide to rip, here are two ways to do it.

One stitch at a time
In this method, commonly known as unknitting or tinking (knit-ing spelled backward, sort of), you rip out one stitch at a time, which goes slowly, but there is little risk of losing stitches.

To do this, first turn your work around (for example, if you're working a purl row, turn work so knit side is facing you and working yarn is in back). Then insert your right-hand needle into the stitch below the next one on your left-hand needle (as shown above) and pull yarn to release stitch. Repeat until all unwanted stitches are removed. Turn work back around to restart knitting.

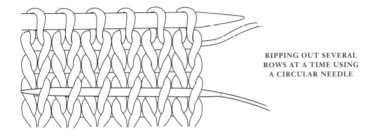

RIPPING OUT SEVERAL
ROWS AT A TIME USING
A CIRCULAR NEEDLE

Several rows at a time
Insert a small circular needle (meaning a circular needle with a small diameter, not a short circular-needle) in your knitting where you want to restart, placing it under the right leg of each stitch in a row (as shown above). Alternatively, if you find that the circular needle is not flexible enough to snag the right leg of each stitch, thread a "lifeline," a piece of smooth, thin **WASTE YARN**, such as crochet cotton or dental floss, through each stitch at the bottom row of the section you want to rip.

When you have all the stitches in the row on the small needle or lifeline, slide the loops off your working needle, and pull the yarn to unravel the knitting down to needle or lifeline. Double-check the number of stitches you have, and make sure the stitches are mounted conventionally on the needle, its front leg slanting toward the needle tip (*see Mounted*).

To Rip or Not to Rip

Should you rip it out or not? For those moments when your needles hover over a piece of work, undecided, consider the statements below and take appropriate action.

When someone compliments me on this scarf I know that I will say, "Yes, but there's a mistake…" and I will point out the error.	Rip it.
I may not say anything to anyone, but I will think about it every time I put this on.	Rip it.
I would not presume to create anything that is perfect; only the Creator can do that, so I leave errors unfixed as a way to show my respect.	Leave it.
I goofed and most people would never know unless I point it out. In fact, I'll probably forget it's there in a few months.	Leave it.
Spirit enters a handmade object by way of an imperfection. This "mistake" is actually a pathway for spirit to enter the work.	Leave it.
I love knitting. When this project is done I'll immediately start another one. If I'm going to be knitting anyway why not re-knit this one?	Rip it.
This pattern is complicated enough to knit in the first place, never mind getting it back on the needles after I rip it. The mistakes I may make trying to fix this could be worse than the original error.	Leave it.
Flip a coin and see how you feel about the answer you get.	Let fate decide.
None of the statements above match how I feel.	Put the knitting aside for a while.

Worksheets

A journal or collection of worksheets can help you keep track of your knitting in case you have to stop in the middle of the project. If you like a project or a particular technique, keeping a record will enable you to reproduce it.

Some people keep a bound notebook for this purpose. If you use a three-ring binder, you can also insert plastic pouches to hold the swatches with the pattern, as well as a photo of the finished object.

On the following pages, you will find worksheets that you can copy for your personal use to help you plan your projects and keep a record of the decisions you have made.

Types of worksheets

Project worksheet

A record of general information about your project: the yarn, the size, and where you got the pattern should you ever want to make it again. Staple yarn labels to the worksheet so you can review the yarns' recommended washing instructions when needed. Staple your receipts for yarn purchases to the worksheet too, in case you bought more than you needed and are able to return it to the store.

Planning worksheet

On this worksheet, make specific notes on how you plan to make a knitted piece. That way, if you want to knit it again or have to put it down for a while, you have a record of what decisions you made at the outset. This is particularly useful if you are making two of a kind, such as socks or mittens.

Schematic worksheet

This worksheet gives you a place to record the number of stitches you are supposed to have at various key points when you are making a sweater so that you can easily check your progress as you go. If desired, adapt this worksheet by adding other check-points you feel are important or to accommodate other types of projects.

Project
Worksheet

PROJECT:

DATE STARTED: DATE COMPLETED:

NAME OF PATTERN:

SOURCE OF PATTERN:

NAME OF YARN, FIBER CONTENT, AND DYE LOT:

QUANTITY OF YARN ACQUIRED/USED:

NEEDLE SIZES USED:

STAPLE RECEIPTS AND YARN LABEL HERE

GAUGE:

CHOSEN SIZE:

RECIPIENT OF FINISHED PIECE:

NOTES ON ALTERATIONS TO THE PATTERN:

OTHER NOTES:

Planning
Worksheet

PROJECT NAME:

....

1. CAST-ON

ELASTIC ☐   FIRM ☐   METHOD CHOSEN:

....

2. SELVEDGE

☐ ALWAYS WORK THE FIRST AND LAST STITCHES IN PATTERN

☐ ALWAYS KNIT THE FIRST AND LAST STITCHES

☐ ALWAYS WORK THE FIRST AND LAST STITCHES IN STOCKINETTE STITCH

☐ ALWAYS SLIP THE FIRST STITCH AND KNIT THE LAST STITCH

☐ WORK _____ EXTRA STITCHES FOR SEAMING

☐ OTHER

....

3. INCREASES/DECREASES AT SELVEDGE

☐ MAKE INCREASES AND DECREASES AT THE VERY EDGE

☐ MAKE INCREASES AND DECREASES _____ STITCHES FROM EDGES

☐ OTHER

....

4. ALTERATIONS TO DIMENSIONS OF PIECES

NOTE ALTERATIONS TO LENGTH AND/OR WIDTH OF PIECES HERE:

....

....

....

....

....

5. COLORWORK

MAIN COLOR:

....

CONTRASTING COLOR(S):

....

6. NUMBER OF STITCHES TO CAST ON

NUMBER OF STITCHES REQUIRED FOR CHOSEN SIZE:

....

NUMBER OF EXTRA STITCHES ADDED FOR SEAMING, ALTERATIONS, OR PATTERN REPEATS:

....

TOTAL NUMBER CAST ON:

....

7. TYPES OF INCREASES AND DECREASES USED

PLACE	INC OR DEC TYPE
PLACE	INC OR DEC TYPE
PLACE	INC OR DEC TYPE

8. BIND-OFF

STRETCHY ☐   FIRM ☐   METHOD USED:

....

Schematic Worksheet

PROJECT NAME:
....

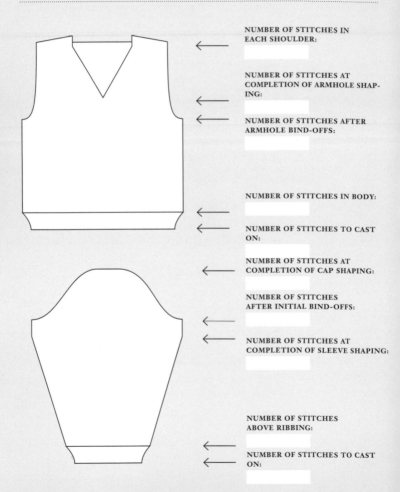

NUMBER OF STITCHES IN
EACH SHOULDER:

NUMBER OF STITCHES AT
COMPLETION OF ARMHOLE SHAP-
ING:

NUMBER OF STITCHES AFTER
ARMHOLE BIND-OFFS:

NUMBER OF STITCHES IN BODY:

NUMBER OF STITCHES TO CAST
ON:

NUMBER OF STITCHES AT
COMPLETION OF CAP SHAPING:

NUMBER OF STITCHES
AFTER INITIAL BIND-OFFS:

NUMBER OF STITCHES AT
COMPLETION OF SLEEVE SHAPING:

NUMBER OF STITCHES
ABOVE RIBBING:

NUMBER OF STITCHES TO CAST
ON:

US/Metric Needle Sizes

Knitting needles are measured in two ways. The diameter of the needle is the most important measurement and is always indicated in the pattern; the length is less important with straight needles but helpful to know with circular needles. Depending on the manufacturer, needles can be labeled according to the US measuring system or the metric system.

US SIZE	METRIC SIZE (MM)	US SIZE	METRIC SIZE (MM)
0	2.0	10	6.0
1	2.25	10½	6.5
2	2.75	11	8.0
3	3.25	13	9.0
4	3.5	15	10.0
5	3.75	17	12.75
6	4.0	19	15.0
7	4.5	35	19.0
8	5.0	50	25.0
9	5.5		

Metric/Imperial Conversion Equations

To convert between Metric and Imperial measurements, fill in the blanks and multiply using the table below:

IF YOU HAVE...	AND YOU WANT...	MULTIPLY THE NUMBER OF...	EQUALS
CENTIMETERS	INCHES	CENTIMETERS X 0.394	___ INCHES
METERS	YARDS	METERS X 1.1	___ YARDS
INCHES	CENTIMETERS	INCHES X 2.54	___ CENTIMETERS
YARDS	METERS	YARDS X .91	___ METERS
GRAMS	OUNCES	GRAMS X 0.035	___ OUNCES
OUNCES	GRAMS	OUNCES X 28.3	___ GRAMS

Abbreviations at a Glance

KNITSPEAK	SPELLED OUT	KNITSPEAK	SPELLED OUT
alt	Alternate	k2tog	Knit 2 together
approx	Approximately	k3tog	Knit 3 together
beg	Beginning	kfb	Knit into front and back of next stitch
bet	Between		
BO	Bind off	ktbl	Knit through back loop
ca	Circa	kwise	Knitwise; as if to knit
CC	Contrasting color	L	Left
ch	Chain	LC	Left cross
cm	Centimeters	LH	Left hand
cn	Cable needle	LLI	Left lifted increase
CO	Cast on	m	Meter or marker
cont	Continue	M1	Make 1
dec	Decrease	M1L	Make 1 left-slanting
DK	Double knitting	M1R	Make 1 right-slanting
dpn(s)	Double-pointed needle(s)	MC	Main color
f&b	Front and back	meas	Measure(s)
foll	Follow(s); following	mm	Millimeters
g, gm	Gram	no.	Number
in	Inch	oz	Ounces
inc	Increase	p	Purl
k	Knit	p1f&b	Purl info front and back of next stitch
k1f&b	Knit into front and back of next stitch	p2tog	Purl 2 together
		p3tog	Purl 3 together

For a more complete listing of abbreviations and for detail on their meanings, see the entries in the A-Z section.

KNITSPEAK	SPELLED OUT	KNITSPEAK	SPELLED OUT
patt	Pattern	sep	Separately
pfb	Purl into front and back of next stitch	sk2p	Slip, knit 2 stitches together, pass slipped stitch over
pm	Place marker	skp, skpo	Slip, knit, pass slip stitch over
prev	Previous		
psso	Pass slipped stitch over	sl	Slip
ptbl	Purl through back loop	sm	Slip marker
PU	Pick up	ssk	Slip, slip, knit
pwise	Purlwise; as if to purl	ssp	Slip, slip, purl
R	Right	St st	Stockinette stitch
RC	Right cross	st(s)	Stitch(es)
rem	Remaining; remains	tbl	Through back loop
rep	Repeat	tog	Together
rev St st	Reverse Stockinette stitch	W&T	Wrap and turn
		WS	Wrong side
RH	Right hand	wyib	With yarn in back
RLI	Right lifted increase	wyif	With yarn in front
rnd(s)	Round(s)	yb	Yarn in back of the work
RS	Right side		
s2kp	Slip 2 as if to k2tog, knit 1, pass slipped stitches over	yd	Yard
		yf, yfwd	Yarn in front of the work
sc	Single crochet	yo	Yarn over
selv	Selvage; selvedge	yon, yrn	Yarn over needle; yarn around needle (same as yarn over)

Bibliography

Allen, Pam, *Knitting for Dummies*, Wiley, 2002.

Budd, Ann, *The Knitter's Handy Book of Patterns*, Interweave Press, 2002.

Buss, Katharina, *Big Book of Knitting*, Sterling, 2001.

Learn How Book: Knitting, Crochet, Tatting, Embroidery, Coats & Clarks. Book No 170-D, 1975.

Falick, Melanie, *Kids Knitting: Projects for Kids of All Ages*, Artisan, 1998.

Gibson-Roberts, Priscilla A. and Deborah Robson, *Knitting in the Old Way: Designs and Techniques from Ethnic Sweaters*, Nomad Press, 2004.

Hansen, Robin, *Favorite Mittens: Best Traditional Mitten Patterns from Fox & Geese & Fences and Flying Geese & Partridge Feet*, Down East Books, 2005.

Lind, Vibeke, *Knitting in the Nordic Tradition*, Lark Books, 1997.

Macris, Gina, *Start to Knit: From Casting On to Binding Off*, Sterling, 2005.

Malcolm, Trisha (ed.). *Vogue Knitting Quick Reference: The Ultimate Portable Knitting Compendium*, Sixth & Spring Books, 2002.

McGlynn, Virginia D., *Knitting Illustrated: For Beginners and Others*, Abbott Yarn Shoppe, 1990.

McGlynn, Virginia D., *Finishing Illustrated for Knitting and Crocheting*, Abbott Yarn Shoppe, 1980.

Melville, Sally, *The Knit Stitch (The Knitting Experience, Book 1)*, XRX Books, 2002.

Meyers, Belle, *Knitting Know-How: An Illustrated Encyclopedia*, Harper & Row, 1981.

Mon Tricot, *1500 Patterns No 0J84*, Mon Tricot Collection, 1984.

Radcliffe, Margaret, *The Knitting Answer Book: Solutions to Every Problem You'll Ever Face; Answers to Every Question You'll Ever Ask*, Storey, 2005.

Righetti, Maggie, *Knitting in Plain English*, St. Martin's Press, 1986.

Square, Vicki, *The Knitter's Companion*, Interweave Press, 2006.

Stanley, Montse, *Reader's Digest Knitter's Handbook: A Comprehensive Guide to the Principles and Techniques of Handknitting*, Reader's Digest, 2001.

Knitting School: A Complete Course, Sterling Publishing, 2003.

Stoller, Debbie, *Stitch 'n Bitch: The Knitter's Handbook*, Workman, 2003.

Swansen, Meg, *Handknitting with Meg Swansen*, Schoolhouse Press, 1995.

Swansen, Meg, *Meg Swansen's Knitting*, Interweave Press, 1999.

Szabo, Janet, *The "I Hate to Finish Sweaters" Guide to Finishing Sweaters*, Big Sky Knitting, 2000.

Thomas, Mary, *Mary Thomas's Knitting Book*, Dover, 1972.

Walker, Barbara, *A Treasury of Knitting Patterns*, Schoolhouse Press, 1998.

Wiseman, Nancie M., *The Knitter's Book of Finishing Techniques*, Martingale, 2002.

Zimmerman, Elizabeth, *Knitting Without Tears: Basic Techniques and Easy-to-Follow Directions for Garments to Fit All Sizes*, Simon & Schuster, 1995.

Acknowledgements

Donald Stuart Berman for his wisdom and his love.

Annette Annechild for showing me the way.

Richard Price, my gift from the universe.

Eric, Raoul, Jill, Lynn, and Zak for love, music, art, and jokes.

Felicia DeMay Berman for emotional and grammatical support.

Mary and John Price for having faith in me.

Linda Carter of the Yarn Garden for support and encouragement.

Focus group participants in Olympia, WA, and Portland, OR,
for their contributions.

Columbia Heights Coffee Staff Meeting Group for keeping me on task.

Linda Hetzer for bringing clarity to chaos.

Melanie Falick for guidance and direction.

Sarah Von Dreele for her elegant design sense.

Patti Pierce Stone for the lovely illustrations.

JC Briar for technical editing.

Wilson Myers for research assistance.

Michael del Vecchio for sage advice.

Faith Benton, Andrea Brady, Gloria Cohen, Christine Dara, Bani Dheer,
Melissa Mowrey, Sarah Myers, Anne Phillips for stalwart friendship.

Christina French-Miller, a Special Person.

All the folks at NEW-BOLD Enterprises, Inc. for their patience.

Thanks to Marie Connolly of Stitch DC and all my students for their
patience and their joy, and especially the student who said, "I look at
the pattern, and to me, it's Knitspeak." You are my inspiration.

In loving memory: Kip Miller, Edith Miller Berman, Walter Benson Miller,
Sophie Klein Pressman, Darlene Ritter.

Andrea Berman Price is a lifelong knitting enthusiast and part-time
knitting teacher. She is also a Washington, D.C.-based project manager
who makes a living organizing complex Governmental programs.